Lynn Buckle was educated at University of Warwick and NUI Maynooth as an art historian and tutor. She lives on the boggy hinterlands beyond Dublin with her children, large and small. She draws, paints, and teaches there. Her protest writing features in *HCE Review*, *Luisne an Chleite*, *Brigid*, *Infinite Possibilities and the époque press é-zine*. She has benefitted from awards by the John Hewitt Society, Greywood Arts, Kildare Arts & Library Service, and was appointed UNESCO Cities of Literature Writer in Residence 2021 at the National Centre for Writing, Norwich.

Lynn's debut novel *The Groundsmen* was published by époque press in 2018

Lynn Buckle

WHAT
WILLOW
SAYS

époque press

Published by époque press in 2021
www.epoquepress.com

Typeset in Abril Text Light/Regular/Italic
& Aviano Royale

Typesetting & cover design by Ten Storeys®

Printed and bound in Great Britain by Clays Ltd, Elcograf S.p.A.

British Library Cataloguing-in-Publication Data
A catalogue record for this book is available from
the British Library

ISBN 978-1-8380592-8-6

This book is dedicated to Sophia

Entry No: 1

Wind: *force 0 to 7 in ten seconds*
Weather: *fine, dry, which is a jubilant sign*
Outlook: *good*

We struggle to hear in our household. Age, degeneration, aural complications and congenital conditions. Ignorance. We have confusing discussions, mistaken arrangements, and fights over hearing aid batteries. Plus, the convenience of not hearing when it suits us. Now we are trying to listen, to each other, and to trees. There is so much that we have never heard, so little time to hear it. This much is true.

Entry No: 2

Wind: *light air, moving slowly*
Weather: *29°C*
Outlook: *warnings in place*

Granddaughter sits beside me on sun-warmed steps watching the evening progress. It is the same every summer along our street. Children running, friends hiding, catching, escaping, siblings belonging and quarrelling, drivers saluting, pulling home. She signs something to a girl crouching behind hot-metalled cars, turns her head to hear better. There is nothing to hear. The girl is gone. Pavements shimmer.

    she says play   she mouths, chasing after her.

    I am learning to read her signs, signals, body movements, eyes, and gaps in between all of these. Sign language being the least, it seems, of her many languages. I am not a slow learner. Although fifty years her senior I am quite able, within the tyranny of hearing, to communicate. It is just so difficult.

    They run in and out of trimmed hedges, trespass driveways, and hide in doorways. Smaller children join them. Older ones next, imposing order, inventing rank, elevating rules, and demanding adherence. The other girl turns to her and mimes a charade of explanations. Maybe not, according to the laughs directed at her bigger brother making the pronouncements. They may be mocking boys, in their self-made language.

    'Talk properly,' he says.

They ignore it. He tells them that he is - on it - for catch. They wave hands in his face. A toddler copies. Two six-year-olds follow suit and so it goes on until they are all gathered, flapping hands around his head. At his signal, they disperse all at once across the green. She is two-seconds behind, following their movement. The mouthy boy, taller than his trousers, drapes himself over a climbing frame. He counts too fast to ten, while sneaking peeks through fingers. He watches her race behind some wheelie bins, memorizes position, fakes a blind twirl, and heads in her direction. She catches his stamp of feet on concrete long before he reaches her, and she shifts around her shelter. Ordinarily a winning ruse, had he not cheated, and she not squealed.

'Donkey-pig,' he calls her, kicking at the bins, demanding defeat.

She will not be drawn, irking him further. Trapped between refuse and fence, she can only imagine his comments as he bangs against the containers with increasing ferocity. I stand, delay, watch as rubbish finally topples over. Contents and child exposed. She stands, hands on hips, defying his defiance just as the house-holder yells. Boy runs, Granddaughter gets told to pick it all up. I know that she could guess the adult's request, that she chooses not to. She signs something, which I also know she could have said. She makes to leave, saunters even. An arm is yanked, more words, more sign, another child runs into view, explains, points, swear words, and the game ends, for Granddaughter anyway. She heads back towards me, leaving rubbish and a red-faced adult behind. I admire her audacity and ingenuity in turning deafness to advantage. I admire. From a distance.

I suggest a stroll along the strip of grass edging the riverbank in front of our house, skirting past the main arena of children, leading away from the houses. Beech trees tower on the opposite side of the river, foliage bursting through their ivy wrappings, spiralling down to thick walls of mistle, briar, and impenetrable vegetation. There is no passage through such lower storeys, except perhaps for low-crawling creatures whose nocturnal calls bely positions. Wild hiding places spilling into bullrushes and tangled grasses hanging over water, altering river courses every Summer until exceptional rains restore channels. It is low water, but only at this point where it has widened into a slow basin, dampening heat and spawning clouds of midges. They glow against the evening sun and brush against my skin. They do not alight upon her, too fast for their lazy bites. She runs ahead, flapping her arms in imitation of the large heron taking off alongside her. They head downstream, in parallel. The bird's laborious wings soughing, barely rising above the water, it is slower than her running. It decides against flight and makes a cumbersome landing before folding into position. Fraying chest feathers waft, then settle. Motionless, they watch each other across the water, held in ash-grey stares. Bird of heaven. Corr réisc in Irish. Beautiful names behind hypnotizing eyes. Predatory statuary, it waits, it listens. The hearing range of humans is 20 - 20,000 Hz. But child and heron are not on this frequency. Hearing differently, isolated by their bandwidths, they tune-in to each other.

This lone bird without colony or mate, living here these nine years past, owns these parts of river. Shallows for wading, deep pools for fishing, and wide enough to escape from kids on estates. It helps that wooden fencing divides their environments. Parents' fears of drownings steers children clear of these waters. The Anderson's boy being the most recent to go. It was a blow-in family he came from, foreign to these parts. How were they to know about our legends? Ten days of searching before he was found, and even then his mother doubted it was him. He looked different, and not for the obvious reasons. Smaller, she said, with webbing toes. She has not grieved fully yet, still waiting for the rest of him to come home.

Severe warnings continue to be issued of currents, rapids, and circling whirlpools sucking bodies into underground chambers. It's said that children re-emerge down-stream having fed ombrogenous mires with their blood, given-over to uisce to roam the vast Bogs of Allen. Their desiccated bodies blowing in the brown dust sweeping over cut-away peatlands or left floating on rotting waters. Their blackened bog-oak fingers piercing the surface, beckoning unwary walkers into their swamps.

It all began with Oirnín, son of high kings and maternal herons. He was born a bird on water to a family whose bloodline ran as fluidly through humans as it did through its avian partners. They were honourable and protected nobles with fine features and a wing-ed strength. His sister, though, was born to land and disinclined to water. She refused to even dampen her feet in the rivers and lakes of their land. Oirnín was left wanting, with no one to play with. He yearned for her to be always at his side, to glide through liquid with his own deft ease and accompany him in his watery world. So one day he lured her in to the lake, watching as she stepped tentatively through the shallows towards him, until the rush of cold currents pulled her in. She splashed and floundered and flailed and, yes, she drowned, as the concentric waves carried her future from him. He mourned her sorely but dead she was not, for she traversed the waters, slipped through weed and wound past fish, wrapping herself around him as he heron-stepped through the shallows searching for her. The family dredged their lake, re-directed the river which fed it, drained the soil in their search for a body to bury, but they were not rewarded. They caught occasional glimpses of neat long fingers, sometimes black, sometimes grey, and their sharp heron cries would fill the air. Or a feather might be seen drifting against the pull of wind, hovering over the peat, a sign they hoped would lead them to her. But their search was always in vain. When the seasons turned once more, she proved her lineage's adaptability. Having waited long in the denuded puddles of dried-up river beds, she was ready to complete her transformation. The rains had come and as the family sat grieving on the musty banks a frog slid out from a silty aquifer and danced before them. She danced so beautifully, a reel of such note, that it was surely she her family concurred. They laughed and clapped, and she croaked in mimicry of their fine calls as they all chorused her return. Thereafter the royal herons refrained from eating frogs lest they be family too, and no one dared tread the wetlands where spawn was stored, for fear of killing amphibious progeny.

It is for this reason that locals do not traverse their surroundings. Apart from when high summer suns and warm breezes allow for the collective digging of turf, when they venture out with long-handled sleáns and build drying stacks of winter-time fuel. On striking the soil, blood-stained water leaches into newly footed ditches, reminding the diggers of children lost and of mothers keening for waters to return them. And all the while their small ones, who now breathe through their skin, play underneath drains and in sinking bog holes. It all starts with the heron up-river. Do not let him tempt your children, for frogs they will become.

I tell Granddaughter this, pull her head close into my chest so that she may feel the vibrations of my warnings.

'Recognise beguilement, it is as important as swimming lessons.'

We live and walk upon these stories. She, at least, returns to me, having spurned the bird's enticement. I couldn't bear losing another.

Entry No: 3

Wind: *calm*
Weather: *temperatures rising, wave height slight*
Outlook: *tears may cause flooding*

'Alright, come out back,' I beckon, 'we'll do some digging.'

Wielding her metal detector, she maps the garden, traversing imagined grids. Self-taught. The droning buzz and high-pitched signals of treasures nearly found travel up the rod and into her hand.

They said it would aid her other senses, in the absence of hearing. They had never seemed lacking, but I bought it anyway for those solitary moments when her friends tire of one-sided conversations or she tires from guessing their one-sided language. It is exciting, in an anticipatory way. Like waiting for a fish that might just bite, or a bird that might migrate off-course and land right on your windowsill. We take the detector on our walks where I stop to draw trees for an ongoing project. I have a dwindling number of species yet to record, a few more hybrids and "A Visual Compendium of Native & Non-Native Trees of Ireland" will be completed. Illustrations rather than field guide. Granddaughter never enquires about the point of it. For this I love her. I cave-in to her request to dig local, dig our garden. She is building collections of her own but under this heat I cannot wander far on expeditions. The grass has died off anyway, scorched to the point that raking would prepare it for next year's wild-flower meadow. Less maintenance, prettier, biodiverse, great excuses for when mowing becomes too difficult.

A flashing red light indicates she has found something underground. I start investigating at her request, bouncing a spade off hardened lawn.

Stop   she warns.

'Treasure severed?'

Dog   *dead*   *bury*

There is an indentation, a slight sinking. I cannot remember the burial's exact location, what with cats, hamsters, and generations of goldfish. She is getting impatient, hoping for discarded remnants of golden torcs or bronze-age clasps. Not dog collars. Wait a moment, the detector screeches, something else under the surface.

dig

I extract something with a mattock. Knotted in grassy roots, dusted with soil and powdery rust, hides a horseshoe. She looks confused, puts it back, for the black kelpie horses of legend would not like it if she stole it from them. She'd read of their great strength, to be feared and respected. Of how they submerge underwater with flanks fleshed by pike or carp and manes drawn through with aquatic weeds. They might swim up through channels, watercourses, or bubbling floods and even Summer droughts do not restrict their movements. For their bodies change into any species and may take you unawares. May take you with them into floating sediments if you do not read the wave of their tails correctly. If you do not read sign.

She has a strict order for classifying her finds and rights of ownership. Tractor bolts, tin cans, headphone wires, the detritus of towpaths, cannot be shared. They line the patio, awaiting entry to her inventory. A cloth-bound book contains her columns of drawings and symbols, further languages to de-mystify. She shuffles the piles of objects around, clears a paving slab for a new category, and chalks an ogham-like mark. The alphabet of Celts and of those before them. The metal-detecting resumes at the far end of the garden, under bushes and low trees. Sifting through overgrowth and skimming compost heaps. She pushes a rotten sleeper which once bordered our pond, sometime sandpit, now home to spiders, imagined deadly creatures and broken toys. The detector signals again. The dilemma of treasure versus predators. She kicks the beam this time, leaping back and forth in a daring dance until a final jab rolls it over, exposing iron bolts, and she halts. Her back towards me, she crouches to inspect the ground as she signs something. I choose not to understand. She does it again, but possibly back-to-front and her wrists twist and really it is nothing like any proper sign. She repeats the movements with an insistence which, if written, would include capital letters and exclamation marks and fierce expositions. I recall it now from a bedtime story, when she had laid her head against my chest to feel the words being read. Stories of yearning beauties, their hearts bound by metal bands to hold their longing in. I read to her of fruitless suitors and how charming princes were always to be found, listless and waiting, in ponds. By way of explanation I had traced a word across her tiny hand, then drew a picture of it before leaping off the bed to demonstrate.

a frog

We have home sign for that, learnt long before the others came along. She created it herself that night as I hopped about the bedroom floor destroying knee joints and was rewarded with our first creation in mutual conversation.

I pace over to her slowly, scared of scaring, and it is indeed a common frog she has found. Eyes bulging, skin panting, it sits, and waits.

what is your name?

Please don't call it after your mother, wandering where waters still. Don't pull my grief around the garden and leave me hoping for her return.

It croaks.

what do you say?

She cups her hands, encasing its moist flickers of movement, and smiles.

her name is secret   she lives here

She releases it, watches it flip away, then rolls the beam back into place. My heart resumes beating but tears are still escaping. Turning, she reaches up and wipes my cheeks.

<u>*she always lives here, under trees*</u>

She tugs at me wanting to know why I cry, wanting more, always wanting. Frustrated, I divert her, tell her to name the tree, we already learnt it when I last drew them.

sign it   we learn it

She is right, of course. I have not got past the alphabet and spelling my name. I have learnt that there is no past tense in signing, I have not learnt what this means. We have a class this Saturday. I have not been practising, she reminds me. I am afraid of getting it wrong, of forgetting a sign, of causing offence with a sign, of causing offence by making no sign at all. So I don't. She knows more than the tutor who, we discovered, is neither deaf nor a sign language expert. Barely fluent, they passed basic level last year and now support others, once a week, for a fiver each. We all installed phone apps for common terms and were given posters with pictures of hand signals. I couldn't get which way round was correct. Should I mirror, or is that taken into account? No one in our class could answer, not even the tutor. I swore under my breath. Granddaughter lip read that. She does not care which way round is correct, it does not do her head in yet. She signs whatever she feels like, caring not about correctness. She leans her feelings into it, she leans into me and I pull back. Her want is as strong as my reserve. She pushes her losses into mine and I cannot bear the strain. It is easier for me to stay quiet. I do not know how to talk.

'W.I.L.L.O.W.,' I spell on my fingers.

what sound?

'I will listen, then tell you what sounds they are making.'

The word itself, or what the tree sounds like? I cannot describe either sound. I could tell her Latin names, look up etymology, show entries in the dictionary and thesaurus, practice writing willow in different fonts in pen and ink and dip a brush into Chinese calligraphy. This is not what she wants. Nor does she want those pencil drawings, the series of tree drawings going back forty years. It is easier to give her all these than to listen to needs, to losses, to listen.

Years ago I planted willow shoots across my back fence. Transferred them, really, by taking cuttings from the nearby park. The original trees were in desperate need of a shrouding after some poor pollarding had taken place. Basal skirts of saplings had gathered around their trunks, like toddlers bothering mothers' legs. I took six of these. They were the sort of strands needed for weaving into bowers and basketry, young branches that will transplant anywhere. I had discovered this when, short of a cane for my garden peas, I improvised with some bendy willow sticks to create a climbing frame. They rooted quickly and green leaves appeared long before my veg was ready for them. My willows are now twice my height. They wave in the barest of gusts, fail to grow densely, and reduce to spindly messes in winter. I never listened to their year-round chatter, when drawing confined observations to visual rhythms. All those years studying their structures, weights, and textures while missing their inherent languages. I do not know what the breeze brings through them or how their sounds differ to the giant trees growing out front, across the river. They may resent being fenced in a line, pruned severely, thrice yearly, accommodating my garden designs. They do not fulfil their purpose; of screening us from neighbours.

She asks of them directly, what they say.

They reply, with the slightest vibration, not even a hum, so hard to detect even with my ears. I try but the wind is slow to oblige, holding its breath. Not even a delicate branch wave. I must sneak up when the wind is blowing, giving voice. All I get is the dry rustle of summered leaves brushing against my sleeve, looking for the point of our conversation.

'Nothing.'

Entry No: 4

Wind: *no air, moving slowly*
Weather: *fine, 31°C*
Outlook: *likelihood of understanding trees is not high*

Washed-out skies, faded lawns, colours diluted as summer is drawn and stretched by a heatwave. The night was hot, early morning warmer, by eleven it was scorching. We learn to shut doors against heat and wallow through still air. The eight-year-old's feet leave sweaty prints. I try not to sleep. Under the shade of the garden willows she draws. In pale chalks on brittle papers, of sheep in winter snow. Asked why, she says it is to feel the cold better and draws me polar bears at night.

do they have trees in Antarctica?

They might if she has anything to do with it. She feels sorry for the opposing poles, she says, when I explain magnetic repulsion, all that resistance.

'What about the isolation?'

polar bears like that   they can eat more fish

This is just enough to keep me awake. By the time the noon-tide moon and sun share opposite sides of the sky she is in need of feeding. We carry a picnic basket over stiles, across the park, over starched grass, to our usual position. There stands a weeping willow. It is all sweeping fronds and curtained shadow. It has salix babylonica stamped onto a black label on its trunk. We sit underneath, among cigarette papers and cider bottles, and metal rings dug into the ground. She asks me what the tree thinks of the state it

14

is living in.

'It doesn't.'

how do you know?

I want to sleep, not explain anthropomorphic tendencies, or give botanical references from Latin dictionaries.

listen   tell me what it says

I shut my eyes and concentrate on noises. The tree may as well not be there. I hear traffic, I tell her, before breaking it down into cars and lorries going over speed bumps, even a bus, I am getting good at this. Birds too, lots of them, talking to each other. Fighting and chirping and singing. And the river, I can hear that too! I open my eyes to see hers are wide and realise just how much she is missing.

the tree?   again

I expect a swishing sound. Nothing. I pretend, say I can hear suantraí, the music of sleep and meditation. She knows I am kidding, as we lie back and look up through the domed canopy, against the sun.

'What do you think it sounds like?'

insects   and it says 'I hide your rubbish'

'Come on, let us do every tree in the park. One of them must be talking.'

I want to find the stridulations which she imagines, the psithurisms of rustling leaves, their sighs and modulations. If they have them.

I hear nothing.

We go from pine to fir to rowan and silver birch, elder, alder, and larch. From horse chestnuts bearing early fruits to Irish oaks with neat, round trunks. Each of them already features in my anthology of trees. They were smaller then, when I knew even less about identification keys and hybridisation and there were many duplicates drawn in my confusion. She is throwing silent shapes, drawing names for them in the air, her hand movements so much more descriptive than the words we share. Inventions borne of observations. She already knows the slow, steadfast way an oak tree grows or how eucalyptus rushes to the sky in the fight for light, how aspen quivers, and ivy gropes. Our vocabulary expands, at her invention, our very own sign language. I should not build confusion, should adhere to official Irish Sign Language, should be one step ahead, should facilitate standardisation. I don't. She is too beautiful to correct, so we adopt her signs and save learning conventions for later.

Not one tree murmurs during our study. What are leaves for if not stealing sunlight or harmonies from breezes? The acoustics of village life predominate. I hear her small breaths panting through thick air. I fill her with liquids, fearful of fainting and 31°C heat strokes.

She assures me we will hear the trees, with practise.

Wind:	*calm*
Weather:	*building very rapidly, 27°C*
Outlook:	*unsettled, calming later*

'Your hand is broken in three places,' the nurse informs me. 'two of them are old injuries, so don't count. How did you do it?'

'Running up the stairs.'

'Your hooves the wrong way around.'

I consider how many times a day she must address the causes of minor injuries, trapped fingers, snapped bones, and sawn toes, to have come up with this explanation. How many times she must have driven to work, bringing bog myths of watery horses with her, infusing them into her medicine. The kelpie was at fault, in this instance, slipping into my body, causing slips on stairs. Their swinging tail spelling warnings.

do not run

If a horse could sign.

She explains the x-ray, addressing the student nurse with actual technical words and they are off on one, discussing her course, tutors and placements, radiology and terminology and isn't this grand like, because I'm in pain and I never knew about the previous two breaks.

'I need it to earn a living,' I say, 'you must fix this.'

They stop at my interruption - my need for speed.

'Artist and writer. I'm learning sign language.'

'Do you require an interpreter?'

'No, I'm learning for my granddaughter.'

While they discuss my youthful looks, calculate birth dates, avoid mentioning teenage pregnancies, Granddaughter makes some home signs, which we all understand,

paint   no   write   no   sign   no

What they don't know is that I've done none of those recently.

'My ex was deaf,' says the senior nurse, 'only one sign needed for him.'

She sends me to orthopaedics in another hospital, one visited only last week. I drive cack-handed over the flat cut-out bogs, past impossibly sized wind turbines and low-growing trees on stretched horizons. I told the nurses we had a lift.

We wait in another hospital foyer. A vast atrium, all glass, triplicates sound and wraps it in water. Echoes reverberate, adding distance to the panic of patients and relatives. A surgeon treads past in brown-blooded Crocs. Bitter scents of coffee and tense waits for results. A familiar landscape. Architects thought to counter all this by planting a tree indoors, having studied the curative nature of nature of course. A lone silver birch, destined for medicinal purposes, tries to get out. No doubt they thought deeply when selecting this species, betula pendula. And it does pendulate, by bending back down from the glass ceiling, bound by this artificial limitation. Delicate, pale leaves hang, filtering light and distracting from all those hopes being dashed. Pharmacology takes notes on paper-white bark. The tiled concourse circumscribes the tree's growth even further, tightening the trunk in ceramic. There is only so much they can do. It strives to survive, quietly, never meeting one of its species.

It appears in my compendium between a stumpy blackthorn, all ink blots and nib scratches, and the soft powders of a downy birch drawing. Both have left their marks and stains upon the silver birch picture, adding to its textures while taking something from it at the same time. Much like this one.

We often come here to visit audiology, to be told that, "the deaf adder that stoppeth her ear," (Psalm 58:4) hath no cure, after trying combinations of operations and investigations and watery excavations under high pressure. Equating deafness with an evil intent, her ears drew a blank. Instead, she conducts conversations with a chironomy of hand signals. Her gestures fill spaces with an eight-year old's incessance at endless chatter. Visual melodies become in-your-face, pay-attention-to-me, lip-reading, demonstrating, remonstrating, listen Nanny, all forms of natural verbosity. There is no such thing as quiet within deafness. She never shuts up. She talks, partially, too. It's complicated, I say when people ask for the exact diagnosis. Her doctors took years explaining it, longer finding out why, and now we're so bored with other people's needs to qualify and quantify, to measure her against the ableism under their skin, that we just say she is deaf.

And this is where she first met her kind. Three years ago, while waiting along with seventy hard-of-hearing pensioners watching slow queues progressing around auditory canals, she was spotted. A child leapt in front of her, clasping Granddaughter's ears in both hands.

'Look Mummy,' the girl said, 'she has sparkly pink hearing aids, like Lucy's!'

A small Lucy, pulled from behind her mother's legs, was shown to us. The effect was instantaneous. Their sheer joy in finding their tribe woke up the room as they hugged and swung and fondled sides of heads, for they had already learnt that this is where differences sit. They looked complete.

I do not know   there are others?
she signs!

My ignorance grown, I should have known, why did I not even think of this? Lucy's parents and I, we tried not to cry, the children were doing it all for us.

My finger joint, I am told, will remain permanently broken.

Wind: *calm*
Weather: *28°C*
Outlook: *good if it involves horses*

Horses were suggested, for their therapeutic effect. She wanted to enrol where her friends went, ride ponies who drew no difference between their charges. She was adamant about this. It was an unlikely success. The instructor, of eastern European descent, had an exceptional voice and was wont to screech at just the right pitch. Her accent confused the other children but not Granddaughter. It merely served to create a level playing field. Or arena, in this case. I came to learn the terminology. I learnt the sign for horse. She learnt to ride and in her lessons I saw a girl transformed. She steered with heels and read the horse's language and still I do not know how the instructor taught her. She smelt of dung and leather soap and all the while she smiled, waiting for the next session. It was a good substitute for counselling.

Today her mount is a small connemara, aged, and prone to objecting to moving. I don't know its name, all the white ones are similar, and are called greys. It stops at the jump just as they are about to lift, or so she thinks, and she shoots over its neck like a bullet. I think of broken necks and paralysis and stairlifts. But she rebounds instantly to her feet, whips around, and lectures her horse fiercely. It understands a wagging hand and hangs its head nonchalantly. She gets back on and makes it go again. The class applaud and she signs her thanks. They answer with

the hand signals she has taught them.
'Keep hands on reins,' instructor yells.
They carry-on talking.

The word deaf is classified in dictionaries as having meanings such as these:

Inattentive	- insert my expletive response
Narrow-minded	- perhaps hearing people will be less so, after reading this
Unpersuadable	- I am now
Stun	- which jars terribly and maybe that is how the deaf are seen, caught in headlights, while really describing looks on people's faces when they first meet someone deaf and they seem, well, normal
Incognizance	- so unaware, it is used thrice
Insensible	- this is what I become when I read entries like these
Refusing	- to accept this stereotype
Unaware	- but none so much as hearing people
Uncompliant	- you get the idea, there is intent here

However, the word horse is classified in dictionaries as having meanings such as these:

Solid	- can be relied upon to heal
Beast of burden	- to carry those worries
Vaulting block	- as she so amply proves
Power	- to heal
Straight	- to the point
Tail	- used to send signals
Mane	- for crying into
Prancer	- other dancers

When definitions conscribe her, Granddaughter rides them out in circles, inventing and combining new ones. She rewrites dictionaries for all who meet her.

Entry No: 7

Wind: *coastal reports are good, wind force 0*
Weather: *fine at 29°C*
Outlook: *getting close*

Sometimes I wish I had started my compendium of tree drawings in an altogether more attractive notebook. Moleskin, for instance, or on deeply textured home-made paper. How appropriate that would have been. I have heard the death cries of trees. When I ground them down, they screamed in electric blenders. I lifted them out of lignin baths on wire meshes stapled to frames, before flattening in presses. That was in my art college years when I learnt that a wooden deckle won't rust, but paper might. Conservation meant something entirely different back then. Such artisan labours would hold so much more appeal to gallery agents, when seeking exhibitions. Instead I draw inside a small, cheap sketch book, stuck with additions and a few notations. It has been re-bound on more than one occasion, as pages bulged with yet more trees which thickened my forestry collection. Edges furred and folios loosened. I should know better. Perhaps I know that beauty can be found in the ugliest of places, and that is why we go searching for it today, for a tree in unfortunate surroundings, to ask what it would say of an embarrassing postal address or a dirty location. Granddaughter and I head off for a landfill site. No excuses, this is work, I say. After our second drive-by she thinks I have missed the dump. She waves from the back seat

   I see the sign

'I know, trees in ugly places,' I say as she lip-reads me in the mirror, 'but this looks too pretty.'

We park tight into the high bank, frightened by the fierce suck of warm air as cars race along the dual carriageway. Clambering to the top, we stand among shelter belts of ash, silver birch, and white poplar. It is possible to see through these to the dump beyond. Diggers rumble and compress dust, creating new slicks which seep and spread an oily sheen. None of it evaporates in the dense heat. Hot, grey smells hang heavy, pushing the taste of refuse. An artic lorry hammers past behind us. The vacuum blast forces all the leaves to flip and lift, exposing undersides of furry white. It is a brief softening before they relax again into green, against the rubbish view.

'They also do that before it rains, to let you know it is coming.'

rain and lorries

She knew it before the leaves did, had already braced herself against the rumble coming up through ground, distinguished difference between diggers and a truck coming at high speed. She licks the foul air, and decides it isn't raining anytime yet.

We leave the birches to their flapping. This is not where I want to carry out research. Back in the stifling car, the radio sea area forecast speaks of late summers off the coast, from Malin Head to Roches Point, and I long for the beaches in between. For Valentia again. We have our midlands equivalent; a sandy lake marooned some seventy-nine miles from port and seashore. We make a detour on our way to the next dry midland town, whose lime trees I want to frame, our adventure laced with promises of swimming.

the black pines

She refers to the cool forest path we take, and the dark

scary words she is sure are being said.

is it okay?   *you and me*

I assure her that under this weighty heat, even trees can say nothing. Their tunnel opens out to a wide basin of water rimmed by sand. Although misplaced, it does not share the same strange air as the sinister avenue. There is no one here, only the memory of weekenders and holidaymakers held in sandcastle moats and barbeque hollows. It holds enjoyment well. Blue skies float on the lake and out onto flat bog. We came unprepared, strip down to undies and run screeching into the still lake. Soft and loamy, the water soaks us in, sounds and all. I do not fear that she has no armbands, fear not when she is within my limits. She has been taught well and slides around as nymph or tadpole. She glides besides my legs and swirls around herself, making waves and sending ripples across to where reeds and bulrushes grow. Sediments rise, clouding the clear water. But still she dives, eyes wide open. A scare as she remains under too long, then a sudden gasp as she surfaces, and her aqua lungs draw laughter. We swim in tandem to the other side, returning on our backs. A chill runs through channels and we seek the places where warmth eddies. We chase each other out, and chase each other in. I grab my princess of the lake and swing her 'til she flings free and splashes freely. The sun on our skin, we lie on the sand, marooned by bog water.

Far beyond the reach of town and its outskirts, I stop on the edge of a half-baked industrial estate. Plots, grassed over, abandoned when the Celtic Tiger died. Metal structures and an unfinished housing block built too close. The bright sun interrogates every surface, dissolving colour. An ugly beauty. Nothing holds sadness quite as well as concrete. A branch reaches out through an unglazed third floor window. A yawning black space pierced by greenery.

We walk over the dead grasses, matted over bumpy piles of builders' rubble.

'Mind your footing,' I say. Forgetting to face her, it is an unheard warning. She slips and would howl but it's me and not her mother, so she pretends it isn't hurting when her shin says otherwise. 'It's okay to cry,' I tell her. Her hands talk to her legs instead. I crouch to give her a piggy-back, then struggle to stand erect. I scrabble with the extra weight, choked by her arms and the peat dust air. Sweat slides between us. We near the empty shell of flats with a tree growing out of it. Hot-smelling plywood hoarding prevents entry at ground level. Not even graffiti artists bother practising here. She slips down to the greyed earth, selects a chalky stone, miles from its original location, and begins drawing on the boards. She names each section and draws accurate depictions of the trees we have learnt about this season. Oak leaves with knotted fingers and willows weeping scratchy tears. Joining these are wavy musical bars, which could be streams, mycelium, travelling airwaves, anything. I trace them with my finger, want to question her intention.

  ask me   *sign language*

'What is their music?'

She punctuates their staves with heavy choruses. I still haven't mastered her language. I want to tell her it doesn't matter, tell of our ancestors whose ancient words she may never hear, but she would know when love spilled from their conversations. That words are only semantics and feelings can be easily translated. We sing her notes, shout out her tunes, fill hot thermals and forgotten monuments with the voices of hand movements. I conduct upwards, to the tree protruding from a window, pause to let it roar a chorus. Its leaves do not rustle. Or sway. They ignore us on this stillest

of days.
     'How did you get in there, grow so tall in your prison? Are
you too high up to tell us why it took so long to branch out?'
     does not want to get caught
     'Stay quiet,' I advise it, 'and keep your squatters' rights.'

Wind:	*storm force winds expected avg. 56 knots, gusts of 130 kmph*
Weather:	*rapid cyclogenesis approaching Ireland*
Outlook:	*unsettled for felines*

A stormy gust blows my cat in through the window, the frame banging his side. Four hours later and he is still holding a grudge against the unexpected weather front. He used the floor as a toilet, a possible indication that he has suffered some internal injury from the wind-slamming. I squeeze his tummy. He objects. A trip to the vet. On my way I collect Granddaughter from her friend's house. She thinks it cool to have a cat in transit, in a basket. His howling quickens my driving. She strokes his neck and feels his straining vocal cords, knows he is upset. I tap the headrest, my signal that she should listen.

'Don't touch him,' I mouth at the rear-view mirror.

he is ok

She coos at him instead, in other-worldly incantations of lisping rhythms and lilting threads. Soothing with hypnotising repetitions, evoking rosaries or Tibetan monks' prayers. It is the most beautiful language I have ever heard, a healing chant which cannot be learned, unless love drives the lexicon. She paints her wavelengths with tonal frequencies rarely used, re-tuning bodily rhythms with her resonances and vibrations not yet measured. By the time we reach the veterinary surgery, she has rearranged his brain chemistry. A check-over reveals no serious injury.

'What class are you going into?' Vet asks.

'She can't hear you.'
second class
what is your teacher called?   He signs
ms fogarty
is she nice?
yes
 you have to say that   *your cat is alright*
She had told me he would be. She tells the vet this, that I
would not listen.

I suggest your nan buys a cat flap
'That will be forty-five euro,' he says, and I want to give
him two hundred for communicating with her like that.

Wind:	*calm, smoke rises vertically, frontal systems moving steadily*
Weather:	*dry*
Outlook:	*but not clear after dark*

She makes our sign for garden willows, expects me to follow her and translate their jostling. Perhaps they are out of my frequency. Or quietude is their preserve. Their personality is not consistent with their messy appearance. They have grown vigorously, and there is ample for harvesting. I cut a handful to show her how their shoots can be woven, bent into slaths, and built upon to create something useful like baskets or wicker fences. I strip bark from a pliant length of willow, as I tell of female strength weaving itself into basketry. Of generations tying-in the first star which holds our creation together, as we thread between spokes, my hand guiding hers, under and over and round and round. How wicker needs love and stores it for years to come. We bend the ribs, up-setting the basket, to create the twelve uprights, the twelve mother goddesses. Here is Danu of the Tuatha Dá Danann and Bóinn of the rivers, there stands Brigid of Imbolc, of Samhain, of all the solstices and equinoxes bringing us circles and cycles of life. Beside her walk the many sisters, supporting the walls. We need more lengths to wrap around and join them, splicing and packing them close. She takes our basket into her own hands, continues weaving deftly. Making without any need of guild, apprenticeship, or worshipful company. Making sisterhoods. She runs a finger over the newly bound waves, explores furrows and creases where sap still leaks, and she knows the shapes her words will take in sign. It is so much more than basket, container or pot. It is all of us stitched together in one fluid movement of woven air and hands. I tell her she has taken back five hundred years.

take what?

'The regulations imposed upon our craft when aldermen, yeomen, any old men of yore who decided trades were theirs and built rules into patterns and licences where love should have been.'

She places the little basket on its side beneath the willows. For the frog to shelter in, she says.

'It is the best home she could wish for.'

She prevents me from stripping further rods, to make another.

do not cut the willows   it is done

They stay out of the conversation.

They said nothing thirty years ago either, at an Irish ashram I once stayed at. I found refuge in the basketry, where tantric yoga meant free labour on tap, and I wove worries into salix caskets and soaked willow osiers in slow streams. There, silence was of religious significance and being deaf was the opposite of not hearing. If words were used they were generally as Gaeilge and whispered in chanting prayers of invocation.

They carried on the air, like summer evening conversations in distant back gardens.

Tonight we have barbeque smoke and the 7 pm refrains of lawnmowers. No hymns to spiritualism, just everyday sounds sinking into dead heat, as they meet hot currents rising from stone, and float on sun-cream slicks in paddling pools. These are my sounds now. To the forest we must go, to hear what is being said in there, and see the shapes they make. We have more than one agenda. There is also the cool pleasure of walking in borrowed shade and the promise of sighting bats, emerging later. We will take provisions, just in case, on our night-time adventure. Marshmallows, which she will have eaten by seven thirty.

We walk against the sun, against silhouetted visitors leaving, and head off-path towards the canyon. Stepping on hot-smelling bracken, the loam and humus crackles. It should be damp, humid, midge filled, not dried like good kindling. It is not just a lack of rainwater. Management have been felling, thinning trees. Piles of shavings, stumps, and discarded foliage surround the hollow canyon once overhung by their branches. Those which remain are no longer straining against each other but against themselves to survive this unseasonal intervention. Below, woodruff, celandine, and avens, have all shrivelled under the harsh exposure. The ground around the crater rim is now polished smooth by human and animal traffic. She runs down the slope, gathering speed to take her up the other side, to where ropes would have been, had her playground not been cleared.

the badgers?　　　she asks of its residents.

Their setts are the cause of this crater. Years of digging, extending tunnels, homing generations inside brocks, have led to structural collapses. The badgers continue to scrape away, creating new entrances of gaping black mouths leading to deeper chambers. It is ever evolving.

'They are still here,' I point to the furthest outpost, site of fresh excavations.

is anyone in?

'Asleep.'

see them on way back　　　at night

The bats had better be in. Too early for their flights,

I wait in the pre-twilight upon a trunk which crosses the hollow's floor. Close to my feet, grey stones encircle a firepit. The ash looks recent enough and the soft grey powder melts between finger and thumb. Granddaughter sweeps past on yet another run-through, speeding towards the other side. Her momentum stops half-way up the steep slope and she is forced to stagger back down and try again. I catch her mid-run and wipe ash onto her sweaty forehead with my right thumb. It sticks like a priest's sign of the cross, half complete. She licks and dips her little fingers into the ash pit, transfers dust to my cheeks in two long pagan streaks, and runs off making primal squeals that are neither noise nor sound you would recognise, unless you had this child. We gather kindling, get a fire going to roast our marshmallows, but she gets distracted waiting and gathers leaves instead. Last year's veiny skeletons, this year's recently fallen, already crisping. She crushes them into her pockets, to press between paper later, as I did in the heatwave of '76. She may also keep her leaves for decades, but I doubt it.

'Sit beside me.'

We lean back on our log, looking out over the perimeter at treetops. We identify four species of trees, first using their English names, then proper Irish sign language ones (of which we only know two). We agree that her made-up versions of sign are best, despite the appealing botanical name for beech in Latin, which is fagus. We try it out, stretching our mouths to see it being lip-read. It looks nothing like the ugly word you imagine it to be. Visually, it begins reticently, opening out into a broad happy word, just like the coy joy found in beeches' own summer leaves. I listen-in to the noises the trees are making, correlate sound with twig movement, look for their sign language in the sweep of leaves as they furl and turn. The best I can come up with,

'A wind is blowing overhead, it sounds green.'

Of course, she can see the wind is now blowing overhead, is already looking at leaf colours, which are bleached insipid greens compared to their former spring palettes. She sees something else turning. Sugars absorbing, waters evaporating, vapours being sucked from the trees. Their trunks vibrating with ultrasonic screams as their thirsty structures endure drought extremes and their roots find nothing. I don't need to tell her of these internal mechanisms.

She knows.

She knows with her eyes from aggregated years of using insides outsides intuition, and times spent concentrating while others went on ignoring her.

She snaps upright, startled by the log. I hear the cause of her alarm a few seconds later; a slight whirring sound. She screams at an enormous stag beetle flying laboriously away from the rotting timber. Its wings struggle against the weight of its long black body, barely able to stay aloft. It is so slow.

the babies!   *hundreds of babies!*

Parasitic mites form a moving swarm beneath its undercarriage, so many that they drip from their host. It is aiming towards the light, or heat, of the fire. We watch in horror at its slow progression.

save them!

'I'm not touching that.'

It draws towards its inevitable ending, landing upon a grey rock within the fire circle. Babies, mites, drop onto hot stone, popping in a series of miniature explosions.

pop corn

She grabs two sticks to scoop the beetle out, flinging it across the hollow as we dash in the opposite direction. We stand, rooted again, and she moves her hands in such a way as to describe the awful flavour of our experience. I do not have the words.

After damping down the fire, we head deeper into the woods. Along paths converging, splitting, missing arrows giving directions, and confuse circuits on maps with tracks going back to where we started. This is not the way to enjoy it. Exertion, weakness, and a rising heat are threatening to curtail our trip. I am much too warm. Granddaughter shivers as we pass the site of brackish water, twice. A black pond oozes there all winter, never tempting children to jump or splash in its dark mirrors. The summer ground has sucked its moisture back, leaving floating lakes of spongy mud. It smells of guns and compost bins. It is touched by branches which should be growing upright, and flies crawl out of suspicious gaps. One year it erupted, pushing out a length of ossified bog oak like a splinter from a pus-filled palm. No one took its offering, buried four thousand years ago. Not even our local craftsman, who is fond of transforming these pieces into golf club prizes and garden ornaments. No one wants to be drawn into that.

She clings to me now in the dimming night, afraid of what she cannot see. We are not the only creatures moving here. Squirrels, mice, foxes, hedgehogs, muntjac invaders, all are stealing through trees. Neither of us can hear them. The ways of woodland residents are much too similar to pookas and hallucinations. Imagining their dirges sets us walking quickly. It is the time of bats, but not owls yet, and the scent of garlic crushed underfoot. We are nearing the clearing of Bord na Móna ruins, housing a colony of pipistrelle bats. Once home to hundreds of transitory workers who harvested the peat to feed our power stations, heat our houses, and supply garden centres. Dormitories, canteens, social halls, all decay slowly in the half-light. We can see the white-washed walls glowing through the tree trunks, casting brilliance across asbestos barracks and abandoned forecourts. Moths and their ghosts are drawn to the glare. Standing at the edge of the encampment, we eat the forgotten marshmallows and wait for bats.

'Eat quietly, you'll scare them off.'

I always eat quietly

'You never do.'

talk quietly   in sign

Something flits across my peripheral vision. Then another, and another, and I eventually attune to the bats. She can't see them yet; thinks I'm making it up. That is, until a thick stream of bats exit their roost and blacken walls as they pour over the glade in their thousands. I tell her about echolocation. She decides she will adopt this method and bounces her imaginary soundwaves off trees until the naked stars can be seen, and the bats cannot, due to darkness.

To get home we could use the short-cut to the car park, which would avoid re-tracing forest paths in the dark. It requires walking through the derelict camp, would take a mere two minutes, and a jump over the odd fence. We both need persuading. We both need a grown-up. The alternative is equally unnerving

deaf bats might fly into my hair

Entry No: 10

Wind:	*high pressure*
Weather:	*rain*
Outlook:	*noise*

When Summer breaks, showers spill on dusty paths and petrichor fills the air. It is a perfumed essence, I tell Granddaughter, dripping from the veins of ancient goddesses. She dabs my forehead freely with their scents. Behind her ears it goes, pulling forth magic, to hear the smell of rain she says. It leaves a muddy stain at the place where cochlear implants may one day go. A letter came with the rains, confirming the offer of surgery. We talk about the possibility of constant interference, of all that hearing, but not about the loss of what she has. Or of any losses really. We had tried explaining to the specialist her many ways of listening and talking. How arms become branches and dance to her emotions, and how trees copy these and all the ways we communicate, making-up our own signals and conversations. That what she has is beautiful. He pointed out that I still haven't learnt the flat-handed jerks of his sign language. Who did I think I was, limiting her connections? She cried then, in the dull silence of the sound-proof room, understanding fully without having heard a word. Was cross when he refused her one of those new hearing bands. Even I could see the point of them. We had looked them up, bespoke head bands, hair accessories decorated in applique flowers or ninja turtles, frogs even, and an amplifier secured inside. She had wanted the camouflage bandana, so she could hide in the trees when playing chase, or a matte black hi-tech bone conductor for secret missions. He said, with the implant, there was no point yet. Next appointment in six months' time. May as well have said never. I sought a second opinion, which differed. None quite matched hers. Still, decisions need to be made.

can I take it out?

'No.'

how do I put batteries in?   will it hurt?   will I hear everything?   where do they put it?

'Where your gills might be. Bottle-up that ichor.'

I don't want it

Her specialists may hear her not, because her ears are not working for them.

She prays it does not rain again.

Entry No: 11

Wind: *calm ⊲1 knot, moving slowly*
Weather: *soft precipitation*
Outlook: *moderate to poor so I turn instead to memories*
             of coastal reports from Valentia

We pause at the front door before walking, on the first day back at school. Watch frantic neighbours pile kids into cars for one-minute trips, wait for engines to subside, and for early morning sighs of carbon monoxide to settle. The rain softens, landing nowhere.

Granddaughter points to the large trees opposite, the beeches and occasional oak banking the river. Their leaves have been disappearing these last few weeks, slowly exposing differences in filigree structures. I have drawn these more times than I can remember. I know each junction, fork, split, and separation, the distances between them in three-dimension, and their heights, relative to my position. Their ages, I know not – two to three hundred years? Some so old I expect Gregorian chants to rise from the stone ruins within them, although a tannery was originally sited there, on the wharf. Stench, then, seeping from the timbers supplying bark tannins, of dead skins, and of all the disgusting things used to cure them.

shut your eyes   listen   trees

I do as she says.

'I can't hear the rain landing on them,' I tell her, 'just the sound of dripping off twigs and branches.' She isn't sure what I said, maybe missed a bit and improvised with the lip-reading.

shut eyes again!

'Landing...it is the sound of many drops of water landing, from a great height,' I tell her   *tall*   I sign, having been taught that gesture due to my stature. She smiles, rewarding my effort, 'and when the water falls it is fast and loud, more urgent than rainfall would be,' I add flamboyant hand movements to show the swollen colours of rapid sounds.

I do not need to know what water sounds like   I know it

'Riveryishness?'

made up word

'Alright.'

Already the fine mist slicks hair to her skull, like a horse had licked it. Indar lat is bó ro leláig. I try to translate it into sign, revert to stroking her wet cranky head instead. I may have signed cow instead of horse. She recoils, at either kelpie or bovine tongues. But it is our mother tongue I want her to own, to freely throw-in an Irish phrase to supplement the other ones. She has so many languages, why not this one?

As we continue our journey, she asks me to identify a tree, newly planted to commemorate a politician's visit. I need a field guide for this specimen, with its blue hues and fancy droop. It looks vulnerable, a lone exotic on the grassy patch between off-licence and betting shop. Small and sheltered, it has no wind to make noise with. I guess its eventual height and spread will outstretch the narrow space, if it survives that long, to pull breezes down through branches, to voice its tunes. That will be Granddaughter in twenty years' time, waving her arms in the air shouting in sign, *look at me, look at me,* commanding attention just like her mother did when she danced on the stage. I watched her edge in front of the chorus line, upstaging soloists who tried in vain to emulate but their feet found no purchase and their arms lacked her grace.

A wooden support, tied too tight around the tree, is already strangling chances. I run a hand over rough trunks in search of an ID tag. The dignitary's name is easier to find, on a smart plaque already vandalised, lying six feet away.

'It isn't native.'

why not?

'It's a pine.'

why can't it be native?

'It's pine, alright? We'll look it up later.'

She touches its silver-grey needles.

get a library book

'We'll go after school.'

She feigns a botanical inspection in the minutiae of whorls on every branch, buying time.

'Come on.'

Instead, she loosens the rubber strap which embeds tree to wooden support. Then stoops to retie laces on new shoes, leaves them loose, feigns another attempt. Eyes averted to avoid my chivvying, she then re-arranges school bag straps, and is about to empty her lunch packet and perform other serious delaying tactics when I extract two metal spheres from my pocket. Chinese worry balls I think they are called. They make a pleasant clacking sound, or vibration in her case. I bend down to hold them close to her hearing aid, gently tap them together, just the right pressure.

that tickles   do it again

She even turns and smiles.

'For you to keep. For school.' I give them to her, with the ornate silk box they came in, her name inside the lid. They tickle her all the way to school, across the road, in through the gate and up the yard to stand in line, shortening the wait as girls gather around her to experiment. It tickles all their ears just the same.

Her new teacher has been informed about the hearing situation. Granddaughter worries that messages may or may not have been passed-on fully, although her photo will have been added to staff-room charts of pupil conditions. From nut allergies to interfering parents, they all get listed. She remembers being told to listen, the mortification of extra tuition, and a new girl's cruel words. Those three things have heavy listings. Sometimes there is no one so deaf as a hearing person. But even though she has tired of reiterating how she may be accommodated her classmates often do it for her. Informing each other to talk slowly rather than loudly, they will swing her about to ensure face-to-face communication. Give her a prod when teacher asks a question, a poke when she really is just daydreaming. She exploits that but is not let away with ignoring home-work listings. They have direct loop systems linking hearing aids to teachers and yes, she may neglect to connect, or dongles may not be operating. She will try to sit with her back to the board or sneak to the back of the class where status is determined. Teacher insistent that proximity matters. It does. They all know she is deaf. So much so that they all forget, which is the best position to be in. Despite all this she might still come home crying, tired from the effort of trying. I cry too. Too easily. The empathy is not effective, only worsens her sorrows as we try to catch-up at home.

I have something important to tell her today when she returns. So important that I have been sorting and assigning old belongings, making preparations in accordance with my news. Blind to the mess, she informs me that she does not have homework. Again, this may not be the case. I decide they don't get homework on the first day back. She tells me nothing about her day, hurries outside to play, a metal ball in each fist. I continue clearing the attic, bringing down boxes and rearranging their contents. I label them with black marker, end up putting some back. I have just one sack of rubbish. I turn my mania to the bedrooms. There is a great deal more to turn-out. She comes in wanting tea, but I have skip-loads of clothes to transport downstairs. She carries a bag of Action Men and Barbies, puts them back under her bed. I build a tower of my writing books and diaries on the landing. My collection measures up, at knee height, plus the supporting research in thirteen file boxes. Next to these skyscrapers teeter multi-storeys of sketchpads, source material for the compendium, and a helter-skelter of photo albums. It is a high-rise postcode of creative living, hastily moving towards the bin and outside. An indiscriminate pile of rubbish now covers the entire front lawn. She is picking through it, extracting pictures. Of her mother's graduation.

what is this one?

'A go-kart, your mother's twelfth birthday,' a tree; Glendalough on the day her mother passed her driving test, two kittens; her mother chose them (we've one left), our old house; the house her mother was born in. When even two parents never seemed to be enough. If I had known then the shortness of their days, I could not have treasured daughter and husband more. We tried having other children, to add to our joy and were spoilt, it seems, so that time had to take some back. I see him in all these photos, although he is in none that I would discard. He is framed many times about the mantlepiece, but here he is behind the camera, on the beaches, building the lean-to studio, digging, mending, repairing, walking alongside me and then...then he wasn't there anymore, and his absence really was an absence and I blamed his heart for giving out too soon and anger filled mine instead of love and my treasures sparkled less so. I wanted to go back in time to the slate mines where, on our first date, we stared up into the light, through dripping caverns, where he unbalanced my mind, and I hoped he would love me. I wanted to re-live all that, to have him all over again. That is, until the memories replaced my pain and I carried on living for our daughters.

All the photos get brought back in, along with a couple of old shoe boxes, partially hand decorated. Too tatty to catch her eye, too rich for me to discard. They date from the nineteen-nineties, when the annual purchase of children's' footwear meant bank loans or late shifts for late husband while I took kids in for neighbours who had proper jobs and I juggled along, drawing in between the nappy changes, toddler groups, school runs, and disco collections until, I realised, I had no career at all and a studio full of pictures and words. Daughter and I had each painted one new shoe box, while sitting cross-legged on the floor. Mine, inevitably, was swept with the delicate lines of branches, reaching over the lid and around the sides, melting into inky blurs and puddles. Hers a collage crafted of felt and magenta silks, dried leaves, buttons, and beads long-since missing. Just glue spots telling of former jewels. We didn't have glitter then, only at Christmas when she would find, hidden inside stockings, light phials of silver or gold stardust. Weighting the bottom and waiting turn, crouched the ornamental frogs which she collected, now filling these two boxes. I clutch their memories close to me and return them to the house, slightly more puddled.

I avoid telling her the important thing, also the reason for clear-outs, such as they are. It all feels like treading water, getting nowhere. My effort to make things easier for others, for an indeterminate date in the future. I need exactness and order, not vague prognoses and clutter. Besides, new school years are unsettling enough. It can wait. Say I am getting new carpets when she asks about turning the house inside-out. She says we only got some in March.

The library doesn't open on a Monday.

Entry No: 12

Wind: *light breeze*
Weather: *depression as fronts move*
Outlook: *I tell no one that I am at stage three*

A path weaves through the park, from our estate into the centre of the village, creating a short-cut for walkers and school kids. I drive by and see sky where trees have always been. My stomach tightens at the sight of a tractor with cutting apparatus. I stop, get out to watch. A two-foot-tall hedge is all that remains alongside the footpath, although hedge would be a generous description for ragged stumps. Tidy Town bureaucrats will be pleased, they dislike the idea of trees screening playgrounds, think them unseemly, not good scenery, and that we need sightlines into darkened places where teenagers congregate because someone decided that they shouldn't.

The ground is spattered with the macerated shards of trees, and sap bleeds from flayed trunks, filling the air with acrid smells. A park splintered. The council works fast, there will soon be nothing left. The tractor races onwards, its arm lacerating bark in quick sweeps of metal disc. Men in hi vis jackets walk to my immediate left and right, watch me photograph the damage. Nervous, we avoid any confrontation and separate. At the top end, by the bridge, a couple of people are already accosting a workman. His arms are waving. If this were home-sign he would be saying *get lost you mad idiots, there is timber flying!* and the couple's body language, arms crossed, replies, *we're going nowhere.*

It's a disgrace, what you are doing, stop it! They do not read each other. They shout over the rattling sounds of tractors instead. They do not hear.

Do not hear if trees scream when being sliced.

We had watched them being planted, twenty-nine years past. Enormous even then, they had to be craned into place, at great expense. I remember that crowd also being held back, as we marvelled at a forest in the making. Remember the size of the stakes needed and, later, more easing back of black bands which strangled the faster-growing species. I got to know them well, in an everyday way. Not that I noticed them growing, their rings expanding. Like children ageing, familiarity is blinding, especially over five-hundred-year timescales. But I knew what to do, and journey time to school varied according to the seasons. We scoured the ground beneath our trees as their nesting birds fledged, collected fallen blue eggs.

what bird? she would have asked me.

'Blackbird,' then, 'thrush,' or, 'starling,' depending on patterning, 'so delicate, don't crush.' Or we stole minutes kicking through rotting leaves, inspected the internal workings of first snowdrops, then bluebells or sought relief under their summer bowers. Sheltering memories of picking dog roses for my wedding.

understand demands hi vis foreman's waving hands.

little man their stance says back.

I take no action, take a circular walk past them, and withdraw to my car. He said, 'it grows back'. But the smell remains, along with the metallic shrieks of machinery, and images of branches ripping and desperately signing their last words as they were falling. I cannot write of what they wrote in the skies. When trees die, slaughter stays, and their language just a memory.

I take no action, take circuitous routes to avoid telling anyone, and withdraw. He said. 'it has grown back, there are still options.' But the smell of disinfectant remains, along with the metallic shrieks of hospital trolleys, and images of lungs ripping and desperately signing last words as I am falling. I cannot write of what is written in the skies.

I must find some normal, far from here, through high live trees to soothe me from these one-sided battle scenes. Away from the town, away from the guilt that I wasn't that couple. And wishing that I was.

Entry No: 13

Wind:	*force 3 gentle breeze*
Weather:	*light rain*
Outlook:	*husband would have told me to keep going so I go to geo location 53.240894, -7.002146*

In the woods where bats flew. I am relieved that at least most of the trees are still standing. This is countered by fears of walking alone here in daytime - nobody walks here alone. Maybe I should not have come, in my haste to get away from the slaughter in the park. I feel the need for Granddaughter's reassurance. She would tell me to listen, to feel, to watch, to do all this by shutting my eyes. I decide to follow her advice and not depend on sight or local knowledge to find my bearings. Could use GPS, but I start by determining my location by the sensation of surfaces underfoot. The car park gravel loosens my footing. I walk forwards, nervous, bend around the barrier, skidding. It is never slippery when eyes are open. She would describe the gravel path with a flat-handed shaky sign, palm down, making a circular motion then fingers dropping bits, sometimes ending in a flick. Moving on from the forest entrance, the ground feels compacted, earthy, reassuringly well-trodden. Both hands brought together in a slow flat horizontal clap, with an extra nod for good measure. That sign could already mean something else. In context, we will know it is ours. Eventually, I reach some fallen leaves, I can tell because it softens. I hear two wood pigeons flutter out from undergrowth, triggering an overhead warning system. A chain of squawking birds sends signals down branch lines, reducing to twitters in the distance.

A stick falls.

A tweet, here, over there, and the constant low thrum of distant traffic. A dog barks, tied up no doubt by a family all gone out. Or in. It talks through the woods, its echoes answer back. Through blackened, darkened trunks, over bronzed mat. I am still training, straining, to filter this out. To find the voice of the trees and identify their species by their noises. They are saying very little, or I am failing to listen. No Hardy's choirs bending leewards, catching notes. That is, until a single tree caters to my impairment. A downburst of waterdrops patters hard and fast on the path, a youthful sapling off-loading. It has listened to the quickening. A rapid wave passes through the woods, rustling from one side to the other, channelling wind. I am three seconds behind, sensing slowly and only hear in stereo, not of vacuums preceding breezes. How immensely unsophisticated.

To counter this, I brag to myself that were this a visual experiment for my compendium, I would have completed my study in minutes, attuned to the colourations of autumn through paint numbers of Windsor & Newton. I even named a daughter after one of these pigments, epiphanies having once been experienced on roads leading to Siena, as a student in Italy. Bog-flat like my midland home, there was mist of a dawn morning as sun and city rose from the waters and I was hooked into its Byzantine quarters. Now raw cathedrals of a different kind burn memories as I slide between observing and learning.

A plane overhead.

The woodland has a heavy sound. Weighted. A downward pressure surrounds me. It is a loitering place. Here, it is said, a man hanged, and he walks abroad in spirit time.

Imposing his presence, even when dead. If only he found his course to the perimeter, where bog encircles forest, he could slip down into ditch waters and join the others, though children they may be. Men are more likely to be found bound in swaddling clothes and retrieved whole, two thousand years later. De-throned kings, slaughtered warriors, sheep drovers taken in the night. They wait to be disinterred to tell of meticulous executions, their nipples lifted and tourniquets gilded. For they may have been to woo Bri Eile, legendary maiden on the fairy mound of Croghan Hill which rises from the bogs at Samhain and sinks with the dawn, admirers and all. Or another may have caused their slaughter. Either way, they lay in the water with their moss coverings turning to peat as trees grew, fell, sank, and blackened with them. I am fortunate that we had no sons to suffer this ignominy. The thought of them turning into leathered purses disturbs me. We did go on to have more children. Some miscarried, one stillborn. One in the river and two left, now safely flown. Not a male among them, not even the ones who chanced their odds, and lost. We are a female line, held together by sisters, and woven into baskets.

It is easy to forget that this woodland floats on an island above cutaway bogs, inching slowly towards decomposition. That tree roots sink into rising waterlines and that flooding is only reclaiming what has been lost. It is only a matter of time before tides lap around trunks and branches signal for help. For now, their waving fronds offer glorious visuals and aural experiences to record, to read, and to imagine their sign languages. All so that I may communicate them to Granddaughter. So that we may communicate with ease. Walking these woods in the eighteen-hundreds, visiting poet Gerard Manley Hopkins wrote, somewhat dryly for these parts:

Trees by their yield
Are known; but I -
My sap is sealed,
My root is dry.
If life within
I none can shew
(Except for sin),
Nor fruit above, -
It must be so -
I do not love.

And yet I do. It is not our languages which fail us. Frequenting woods and inventing words to describe them, even Hopkins, who delights us with his forgotten shivelight slivers of sun piercing through canopies, cannot show love without the poetry of trees. I too walk his woodland pathways inventing words, mine in sign for a child.

I am recreating velvet with my hands, for that is what the wood pigeons sounded like as they flapped away. Gentle strokes of downy arm hair, Granddaughter arms if she were a bird, wings wrapped around me. My fingers respond in soft flutters and folds which do no justice to the sound or image, but I hold her in my hands. I hear her in the itty-bitty chatter of starlings, thrushes, birds sending warnings of an impending climax, which never comes. How to depict their reticence and expectation in sign language? Facial expression, shoulders, a backwards step? It would be a complicated sentence, as quick as flocks scatter.

I follow the track into a dense hollow. The sound is sparser here, emptier despite the thick woods. It may hold what the birds feared. Or this may be the sound of trees' slow growth before they sink. I create cinematic, slow motion signs which evolve from one steady shape to another.

They are backed by low rumbles from the distant village. These do not warrant signs, if I do not want to hear them.

The forest has been planted in clusters of single species; bands of young shelter belts, stands of evergreen conifers, new oak dynasties, swathes of beech and birch. I walk out of one section and into another of pine. The sound changes in an instant. Not quite dead, just different, muffling and absorbing the rustling of nearby deciduous hardwoods. At last, I can hear the difference. Here the secret talk of coniferous trees is in their collective quiet, bedded deeply in insulating floors of browned needles. Even the pines' cracked bark serves to dampen down and slow the travel of sound. Until the wind arrives. It doesn't so much as slough through these sedentary boughs, as hiss and swish and slither sideways. It hits in sneaky whistles and is gone as soon as I can find it.

If I tell Granddaughter, she can sign all that.

I will tell her too of the mono-planting broken by a rogue oak tree, survivor from previous times when bog men filled and fell upon this landscape. When oak meant more than a name can lend. Doíre in Irish, it was a Sessile native, and our county was known as church of the oak. It was settled by abbess Brigid whose story is older still of pagan sisters nursing spiritual shelters. A goddess co-opted into sainthood, her myths not legends of fiction but of real stories of healing powers and a leader of spiritual significance. She spread her magnificent cloak over Curragh plains, marshy fens, and oaken forests. As far as her hems stretched was deemed her county. She stitched them into protective rooves of oak tree canopies, later abbeys, where she lived and nurtured. They are easy signs to configure by hand.

A fallen trunk cuts across my path, displaying a ray of

shallow roots. It has settled on the ground like an upturned locust. A mere thirty years old, the windblown pine was planted far too close to others. All trees, regardless of size, break at the same wind speed of 94 mph, but it wasn't for this that it lies here. Isolated from its kind, it was ousted, told to 'take that and feed the neighbours.' I listen for a different orchestration. Must wait until winds blow again. Behind me a scythering begins, races up through pines and stops atop the old oak tree which takes its time to transfer the sound. Individuated branches catch it, lap it, twigs and the last leaves clap it back and forth noisily, enjoying the fracas until pines sneak it away and sway before I can say I have heard them. Heard their susurrations. If shelter belts work best when they allow fifty per cent of the wind to pass through, then listening can be allowed to follow suit.

I often search for meanings of sound, of hearing, and their opposites in a thesaurus. Collections of words create compositions of their own, sonatas which stop and start among entries which dance across pages in imitation of sign language or trees responding to wind. Florid or faint, discordant words fighting against harmonies, and stridor's shrill constrictions. I draw them out as branches swaying in sign language, altering pressure as pencils trace around definitions, creating speeches with their forms. I do not know what I hope to achieve by this when sign lessons would suffice. I only know that it angers me that deafness follows hearing, and silent comes after sound. So I re-order priorities, cut phrases from dictionaries and rearrange them as leaves until faint becomes strength and loud has another voice.

I still have no image for the scythering of pines. They are locked into papers, made from their pulped trunks. Such inharmonious endings, squeezing all the wind from their folios. Until I recall that musical scores are written on sheets and that crochets and quavers can pull rhythms from paper quires. Just as Granddaughter does when she commands the piano keyboard, imitating the practising of scales. She gets locked in battles over pointless sounds she cannot hear. She always hears the discord...frustration not needing any words.

The leaves were very late falling this year, hung-on until pushed, everyone is saying. It is written into books that beeches will do this, hold their dead in marcescence. I wish I'd had that chance, to have cradled my adult daughter, to have been blessed with her face one last time, many times, for as long as it took to let her go. Instead, the river stole her, and she floated away with all the others.

Some trees, however, are dependent on the weather and shed on command. Their language changes as they undress, in the way arms sweep and the sounds they make. So many accents to learn.

At home, I can hear the council still trimming trees in the park, cutting them down to respectable, acceptable heights. No one stays to rebel, the exposure is too great. Like the willows, they keep their quiet.

Wind:	*zero force, smoke rises vertically*
Weather:	*overnight temperatures dropping*
Outlook:	*'what is slate,' husband had stated 'but squashed clay'*

After Summer's long, slow ending which delayed Autumn, Halloween finally nears. With it come the first scents of the season, a confluence of bark, compost, and woodsmoke. Clear night skies lit by wide yellow moons, shorter days, and home-made stew. A gradual sinking back until all the glories have been stolen from herbaceous borders. Blackening frosts, each one harsher than the last, ensure nothing grows, not even the grass. The timbre of timber changes by late October, and leaf shake becomes a sound of the past. There are occasional creaks as limbs knock and trees contract, but mostly there is a sonorous hush. Especially so among our willows. All activity has transferred underground, where mushrooms have withdrawn to their mycelia and electrical signals hijack their systems, passing private conversations between trees. I draw these for Granddaughter who thinks that I have access to these, that hearing worlds are party to subterranean communications. She is disappointed that we are not, although there is some contentment in knowing secret languages exist still unlearnt. She rubs some of my pencil lines away, says they should be grey, blurred for places unheard, not hard and distinct like black ink. I use a 2H lead instead, fine and precise, to draw silvery threads around roots of trees, and use a graphite stick which barely marks the page. It takes on a life of its own, the drawing growing beyond borders of A4 onto further pages and beyond. It becomes a fold-out concertina of fungal proportions. When we are bored of adding to the networks, she takes a chalky pastel, brown in colour, and, holding it sideways, slides it across the mycelium. She sweeps and dives until everything hides behind layers of earthy pigment. This is what being deaf once looked like, she says.

She asks if my husband minded being buried down among the fungus. Useful as it is for decomposition, I remind her that he requested cremation, fearing subsidence of our graveyard might tip him into marshes. Ancient bog-bodies make it crowded. He wanted somewhere with more permanence, with strong memories to hold him. We took the urn and sprinkled his ashes over quarried stone. It was a hard place to leave him, many Octobers ago, in our Valentia slate mine. He had stated, on our first date there, that all bog turns to rock eventually. We built on that premise, getting engaged a year later, and a strong marriage formed of layered bonds. Years compress. I have so much left. And am reminded daily by shipping forecasts reporting from Valentia's sea areas and I listen to the radio for his name in wind speeds and his place in the waves.

And so it is, on one of these mushroom-smelling evenings, at the time of Samhain and of All Hallows when the dead are remembered, that we join the rest of the village for our annual bonfire, to disguise the dark soundless night with a community of noises. Such gatherings are difficult for both of us, when background sounds of crowds distort everything heard and it is impossible to distinguish words. But now we are armed with sign language. Before we go, we try signing our hands against our bodies, to talk in the dark. It makes her laugh and squirm as my fingers coil around hers and up inside her shirt to write upon her skin. If it does not work, it does not matter, we will stay close to each other. Walking to the field, she starts to have second thoughts, as she has done every year. Fear of fireworks and spectacle, perfectly natural. A ghost walk precedes the main event. To enter, we must walk through ghouls dragging dead spirits along lanterned paths, past moaning faceless monsters to dodge fire-jugglers swinging on trapezes through tree-tops. Beyond these, we are funnelled into a large courtyard, now full of families in costume. Draculas with princess daughters, devils with convicts in stilettos, bandaged pirates eating hotdogs and spilling cocoa. Strings of fairy lights and a blinding 2000-watt floodlight. Loudspeakers blare out music, muffling everything further. In the confusion we do not lose each other, some other signal glues us. She moves, I follow, towards a stone wall dividing crowds from scrubland, where a bonfire has been built. A village has gathered to watch its mattresses burn. A fanfare, then the base is lit. A collective roar. Flames catch and soar through bedding, destabilising cladding, but mostly pallets. The audience steps back and forth in quick ebbs and flows to watch the dangerous pyre fall asunder. Maybe we were ambitious this year, but everyone is in thrall of the danger, their faces burning from the heat. The billowing smoke has settled into a steady plume and as it rises my eyes, acclimatised to the white fire, are drawn across to the voids lying behind it. The blaze-light reaches through marshy fields, to marginal hedges hiding liminal spaces. Imaginations furnish spectral forms in these woody places, invocating calls to those children taken down-water.

A teenager screams.

She muddied her fancy-dress onesie.

A group of men gather beyond the fire, bend and huddle

and trouble each other. Buckets of water are brought. A hand is immersed. Granddaughter checks hers, just as the sky explodes in fireworks. We cling to each other and grin. Then another, then a whole string of bangs and shouts and applause and what about things falling back down upon us? She runs. I have her by the coat as she pulls around bodies and panic slows the collective rush to get away to safety as it rains sulphurous candles upon us. We will be back next year.

Entry No: 15

Wind: *near gale force 7 (NE)*
Weather: *4°C*
Outlook: *the cemetery visits me*

Cold air floods in through the window, bringing with it the sounds of trees. Our trees, as we now call them, across the river. Many noises invade the space between me and the large beeches; distant schoolchildren; planes; traffic; and that incessant pour of water. But I can filter them out now, close off the bloated river's roar and send it westwards with all the other sounds.

This is selective listening. Not the mishearing of the hard of hearing but a skill learnt and earned from hours of attentive listening for dendrology differences. My laurel hedge flaps its plastic leaves, slapping winter-cold sounds. The north-easterly bite, which last night brought with it a thick layer of snow and muffled all susurrations, is now relieving weighted trees and bringing the last molten leaves to ground.

The postman calls and nearly falls backwards when handing over my delivery on the doorstep.

'Damn the imbalance,' he says, 'it's my ears.'

Catching the blame again, as though ears had a choice. I do not give voice to this. Or how having an ear infection is not the same as deafness. I know how quickly hearing aids lose their novelty value, how Granddaughter will not ask strangers to repeat things she has not heard or misunderstood. She depends on context, guesswork, and cover-up. Sometimes laughter when she miscalculates sentences, sometimes she withdraws. Postie is the only adult I will converse with today. I stand holding my parcel in the open doorway and resume listening to what the trees are saying. There is a chaotic wind, creating cacophonies. The insistence of laurel, taking up all the soundwaves. A lone Irish oak, planted along with the estate circa 2002, rustles and shouts at random gusts and I realise it is playing catch with the wind. Hedging claps back.

I shut the door on arboreal noise. My package has been opened by customs, who, curious as to its Chinese origins, have clumsily re-wrapped it and slapped a label over gaping rips. It takes the stuffing out of the joy of gifts. I had scrolled the internet for hours, looking for the perfect metal amphibians to lay at daughter's grave, on the gravel chosen for its green and blue sparkle. Re-cycled glass chippings, they were called, creating a watery pool for the heron to wade in when he stepped from his image chiselled on the grey headstone. The verger suggested plastic flowers, long after the wreaths faded. I couldn't say I didn't like them and neither did she, that she was too fresh for that. He nudged a globe vase into my hands.

'There's a frog inside, keeps them steady,' he had said.

That was when I learnt 'frog' could mean something else and it meant I hadn't forgotten, and tears fell all over again.

'There, there, now. You'll cry so much the kelpies will come swimming-in.'

'Horses have frogs too, in their feet.'

He left us drowning.

Thirteen weeks they took, to deliver my purchases. They are not too small. I didn't want frog-shaped toggles getting lost among gravestone pebbles or cheap trinkets. I had searched through sites, marvelled at auction-house prices for antique frogs and their global appeal. I even open the two shoe boxes. Sort their contents in the order of years they were gifted. It is clear they cannot compare in value. The first Christmas frog she was given consisted of a simple twist of clay, its neck moulded and stretched to gaze at the moon. Raku-fired with a copper glaze, it could shatter outdoors in frost and lose its iridescence. It had been traded for a picture, from a local potter who made several versions, but it was this one which she favoured. It fit every occasion with its smooth shape and surface, fit into school pockets and student jackets and clutch bags, and was clutched during labour, if I recall. But there are others which describe her growing years. The tears she shed when her father died, and that year's gift became a toad and was thrown about the house. The following Christmas wasn't much better, she went off frogs for a little. And after that a cerise plastic creature which squirted water as she reverted. It took the raku to bring her back again. By then she was altogether more sophisticated, and prices did increase. She eyed designer names and frog gifts conformed accordingly. A few years later the frogs took on a bohemian flair which even I struggled to supply, making them in papier-mâché and tie-dying until midnight, being told it wasn't quite right, I should have bought it. That was before the funky ones took over, skateboards and caps, disco sets, and then the retro cartoon sort. By then she was able to draw laughter from her oldest frogs and loved them all again. They clung to windowsills and gathered dust, factory brands, logos, and home-made ones appreciated, but held rather less and nesting now in tissues. I take them out of hibernation to join today's additions.

I settled on two new figurines, finely crafted, which would sit neatly on grave chippings. They survived their journey. The first frog is made of shining gold, with rubies set upon toes and eyes made opalescent by polished turquoise stone. Entranced, I rub the perfect craters on its back, the black holes through which it breathes. Nothing can be seen inside. I bought the second frog out of indecision; it was too beautiful to leave, and I couldn't choose between the two. It owns the ugly word of pulchritude and is not what it seems. Made of frosted glass, with a hint of frozen blue, it is both faded and transparent yet rich in hue. Carved from aquamarine, the only metal bits are the golden rims of its magenta eyes as they stare at you, or the moon. Made by an associate of Carl Fabergé. It changes from water to sky to glacier mint and if I were a drowned child, I would want to be it. I take my narrowest trowel and bury them together under the willow trees, for a detectorist to find. A blue raku goes under a basket, a pink one follows, paired with limited-edition zinc and forget-me-not paint. Paper too, although bound in leather and held by three metal bands. They do not pass comment. The heron cannot have them.

Entry No: 16

Wind:	*an ill wind, at 0 knots*
Weather:	*cloudy with clear spells*
Outlook:	*forget me not, out of season, by wrapping me in paper shrouds*

I rub the notebook full of diary entries about who said what, and why, and when. Making sense of their voices through the curvatures of hand-written words, rather than my first language of pictures. The paper is dry and soft, the sound of cellulose stamped and bleached, pressed into neat sheets. They are empty of wind, sap, inconvenient spurs, or woodlice homed for the Winter. I control the slide and tone of my swipes, add rhythm to my strokes, seeking the lost sounds of trees. I almost hear the rustle of dried leaves as I turn the page, but they are sharply squared notes. I paste one of Granddaughter's skeletal leaves into my book, to soften the sound of the page. It is a fragile sound. The sound of real softness lay in my daughter's voice.

'So soft,' I remind Granddaughter, 'that it did not matter that you could not hear your mother's words, you felt her honey pouring through your ears.'

We remember mead and honeybees and the darling nectar melts our hearts. Just one more spoonful, I need.

I ask for another leaf and she tip-toes around the table with something better, she says, offering up a fingertip. She gifts a tiny forget-me-not from her flower press. So small and blue, a floral full-stop from the summer. I cannot tell her it is nearly the end to other summers too. She lifts layers of card from the small press, marvels at forgotten petals, at how she caught the colour of sun. I take her little finger back and kiss it before it is too late. She glues flowers to my pages until bouquets glow over words and shame my pen. She starts lulling. From deep within lungs, low notes travel up to her tongue, as hypnotic and subtle as any gaelic psalmody. She lulls in rhythmic waves as she pastes her beauties. She softens sounds, softens dead things, composes them differently, drawing me in to fold myself around her and share in her vibrations.

Entry No: 17

Wind: *gale force on northwest coasts decreasing slowly*
Weather: *persistant and heavy rain clearing later*
Outlook: *persistant and heavy cough under the weather*

Granddaughter goes out back to unpack the mystery of what the willows say when they sway. The conditions are ideal, from a meteorological point of view; the rain has recently ceased; and sporadic wind is taking nasty swipes at branches. I join her in the louring afternoon light, stand alongside her on marshy grass, and wait.

'You should wear a coat,' I tell her, 'you've not been right, you'll get a chill in your kidneys,' my mother's memory warns, along with vests being the first defence.

I have two earaches in this ear at the same time

Making everything too loud to hear. For her it isn't clear that crows, beyond and above, circling the darkening sky, are squawking ritual evensongs. Vast numbers converge in the enormous trees lining the canal, fly in and out of roosts, shout collective abuse and yell general discontent about it being bedtime again. Their clamouring protests need recording, to capture their dissonance, to play back in stereo, with added volume through special headphones. To gift what I hear, to her. But she sees their audible screams.

sky fighting

She suggests that, instead, I record the sound of wind through willow. I press record.

Nothing

Nothing but the restless stroking of willow fingers

against lattice fencing. Just a little more scratching would raise the sound levels and provide me with a recording. I put away my phone. The wind strikes back. I take the phone out. Wind stops. In, out, sticks slip, yet they do not clack or answer back. They do not strike or flip or whip against each other in torrents of wind-driven sound-making. The illusive willows say nothing, protected by invisible sound barriers. Granddaughter tries listening for rogue gusts. Through hearing aids moulded into her ears, through the fizz and crackle of miniature loudspeakers, which filter and amplify, and try to make her fit in. They hurt the tiny curves and folds of her skin.

I take my hearing aids out

'All the better to hear them with.'

She signs something incomprehensible.

'What's that?' I ask her to repeat it.

you should know   sign language

'I'm trying,'

She mock applauds in waving sign language. God, just wait until she is fifteen, selectively communicating. Will I ever get to see her head turn away in deliberate refusal to read lips or sign? Will she go out beyond midnight, saying that she missed my constricting arrangements, because she feels eighteen, saying everyone is going, that rules are so mean? I still want to catch her hastening away, catch her when she falls, broken hearted, or gets arrested, gets wasted, gets a degree, and I try to envisage what she will look like, aged twenty-three and me ageing by her side. But I can only imagine her mother, which sets me longing and wishing for things I can never have again, even though they feel the same. I pull a heart shape in fingers, push it out to her. It doesn't reach. She has already turned to stretch through the darkened gaps of branches, to touch a loose fence panel which she had felt thudding, vibrating through watery earth. Her hand is silent in the dark recesses, but another holds my wrist for balance, fingers tracing a sign or symbol whose meaning is drawn into my skin and I am ashamed, I say, I do not know it. She cannot read my lips. It is the hour at which daytime reaches completion, when vision is stolen, and the last warm air is sucked from lungs. My alveoli draw in the cold, shrinking into hardened balls and old scars claw at my rasping breath. Her small arm wraps around me.

Look

Facing westwards we admire orange-red ribands streaking pewter skies, blazing between cleaved houses, lifting the chilling monotones of winter and recent rain. We watch the light slipping from wet colours, until the alchemy is all but extinguished. We have overstayed ourselves in the garden, will soon be freezing. Retreating indoors, we hug kitchen warmth and rub our whitened fingers. She signs sunset followed by her own version with soft-handed fingers spread downwards, head and shoulders weaving, her dance summing up our whole evening. She takes it around the kitchen floor, spreading colour under the fluorescent light and bending beauty around the table. Like the willows, she cannot be recorded.

Wind:	*gale force 9, reducing quickly*
Weather:	*fine sun*
Outlook:	*and so enters the sun as stage four begins*

Last night, strong winds boomeranged back and whipped our ailing fence away. We heard it not in our slumber. Devastation left its tracks, without needing aural verification. Panelling lies across the grass, trees intact. The morning radio says seven thousand are without power, belying today's calm. A yellow glow sinks into the wet garden, raising steam and unseasonal midges which gather in the low sunrays. December's hungry birds blacken the silent willows, taking turns to feast on the insects during quick, successive fly-bys. The cat in turn tries his luck catching birds, leaping aimlessly into their flightpaths. I tempt him away with his breakfast, but he returns to his pastime afterwards, all the more invigorated. This distresses Granddaughter, who also fails to distract him. Sweeping him up, she brings him on our walk. He often follows us, meandering around the park, darting behind hedges when startled, meowing wildly until reaching the security of border territories. The birds have taken precedence though, and he sneaks homewards after just five minutes. Today's constitutional is for research, I tell her, to take photos in today's perfect light. I want to capture the great wall of trees, set far behind our house. Some planted, no doubt, when the canal was first dug, to screen the industrial view for a nearby lord of the manor. Myriads of roots steal water, puncturing limed linings while securing inclines. Eventually banks break, water escapes. Our house, built on the thin strip of land between the canal and the river which supplies it, waits on a flood plain. The beeches, far beyond their end of lives, are gradually falling, or being felled. The gaps they leave have filled with spiky blackthorn, smothered in wayward clouds of old man's beard. I imagine my lungs full of its woolly strands as breaths rasp though infection and alveoli on the make. The gentle fibres spreading until, soon I am told, I will be one large cotton ball. There are other more domestic plants, escapees from gardens, such as an out-of-season out-of-place sprouting forsythia. All those cells over-growing when they should be dormant. The buds should have stayed closed; it could easily snow. In an act of anarchy, to save the planet, the opposite has been happening elsewhere. Ice caps crashing into salty seas, tundras boiling, jungles drying. The drama always somewhere else, until the trees stop budding. She has a teeny-weeny sign for these, an almost flower sign, imperceptibly smaller and tighter, a tremor to her fingers. I try, with my bent and broken digits, to replicate the tremble. A gnarled bud they make. I hold my right hand upright, giving my palm. She flattens hers against it, straight and perfect for smooth, young signs. She feels around my clawed bones, knots her fingers around them.

I can sign for you

She signs to my story of water goddess Bóinn, wrapping her hands around the sounds I make while telling of ancient women who delivered justice from underwater. She interprets key names and phrases, recites in home-sign, flows through flat-handed conventions creating an aqueous language built through years of reciting this tale. I tell her how Bóinn floated from the Boyne, along regional tracts to rivulets feeding our canal, where she was called upon to deliver judgement on an elderly crone, knowledgeable in the ways of plant medications. She had been charged for her part in re-claiming forests which invaders had planted with alien species. She had uprooted them and dug-in her indigenous trees. 'A peculiar theft,' the watery judge said, 'swapping trees for foreign ones.' The invaders, who hailed from the deserts where any tree is luxury, had said it set an anarchic precedent, albeit an arboreal one. Bóinn found the invaders at fault instead, for faulting matriarchal lines. She sentenced them to twenty-one days of removing spruce trees and to build a physick garden for the medicine woman. Her archaic silver birches were allowed to stay. They still stand in small clusters along the gravelled tow path, displaying their white skirts. Their leaves rustle, swing in the last breeze and tell of justice served. The goddess Bóinn swims past occasionally, checking on her restorative orders and compliance with druidical laws. The water serves her well as disguise, while keeping her justice fluid.

Having kept the child from school, I feel no guilt over our excursion. After missing the morning rush we made the executive decision to take the day off. I once set such store by school attendance, such unbending insistence. It has taken decades to relax into parenting, into second chances with third generations. Longer still to see the value of time spent on marshes, telling tales. Along with gentle exercise, which I have been advised is good, and swimming. I have adapted that too, abandoning my rigorous lane training to adopt a more relaxed stroke. Like Bóinn, I steal through the water. Like Granddaughter, I float through my moves. There is no hurry or correct way to swim anymore. My body and blood levels have changed, lungs roughened and burn, so I learn to ignore what does not matter like charts and forms and treatment schedules which sometimes fail and there are always others to try. Like the natural remedies of lost physick gardens and all their modern equivalents. They will lend time to my projects, to her. And what is it, she interrupts, that I write about on our walks, why take photos instead of sketching?

'To have a record of them.'

so, what do the trees say, do you know yet?

'So far, they all say something different. Some speak too slowly for us to hear.'

or fast   like that crack   from   that   tree in the woods?

Last winter, it had let out a shot when frozen water inside had altered tensions and split open old wounds. In that instant, she had felt it breaking via her feet and watched me leap as I had thought we were being hunted. We were nervous for a hot minute. She had mimicked firing a pistol.

I get her to crouch at one end of a fallen tree. Its larger branches have been taken for timber, its trunk awaits dissection. In the race towards decomposition, long, strangling briars are busy burying it.

'Put your ear to the bark.'

At the opposite end, I scratch across the cut radius of rings with my keys. It elicits delight. We take turns sensing each other's vibrations as the wood conducts our messages. She feels sorry for it.

'Don't be, it lived. Now it's a feeding ground for beetles and all those woodlice beneath.'

She insists I roll it over to show her, but it is far too weighty to lift. She looks for spots around it where insects might gather, under mulch and flattened bracken. Digging with a stick she finds a trove of buried beechnuts, stashed by mice and long forgotten. An earwig and some other blackened creeping things scatter away on too many legs, but no woodlice. She picks at bark, pokes rotting timber, wonders where they have gone.

'They'll be curled up somewhere nice and damp, for the winter.'

it is wet everywhere

She despairs and heads over to a large wiry mass filling the ditch between trees and towpath. It is made up of fallen branches and dead overstory scraped into a doughnut-like shape, at least five metres wide. Its walls are, on inspection, roughly woven like a giant bird's nest. Not a basket though, inviting her to play sisterly chases of twisting lath and fitch. She is reluctant to enter the wicket den.

I am not allowed to play in it

'You can, this is everybody's,' forgetting the rules of kids on estates, of lords and flies, and all that entails, 'they're all at school.'

We clamber into its centre, where a rope and tyre dangles. She swings on it for a bit, but is wary, looking from sky to embankment and back again. Permissions being arbitrary things. These trees are full of the sound of kids playing, thoughts of them, despite today's absence.

'I remember your mother climbing this tree when she was your age, when we had just moved here. So good was she at tree-climbing, she just shimmied right up to the top.'

Concerned neighbours would call, insisting I retrieve her, to calm their nerves. No one saw her actually stuck, only aloft, reaching for a large bird which changed from crane to heron to flamingo, depending on the person worrying. I can think of worse things for a child to be doing, fitting in.

tell me about it

I repeat the story, making her ascent ever more heroic, include triumphal flag-waving and a near-death descent into underworlds, riding water horses through Grand Canal channels before emerging to loud applause.

'She wore her blond mane in whorls, tied with purple vetches and yellow daisies.'

can we get her from the underworld?

'One day, when herons decide to give her back.'

but she lands alright, doesn't she, to a crowd of scared parents and everyone is impressed?

'Yes, and she dances in circles and sets so divine, they remember her regal female line.'

everyone wants to be her friend then

I sweep her off the tyre with the invitation of making mud pies and she signs,

I am not five

I take photos, from our low vantage point, of trees in winter's golden hour. A nearly-wind tries blowing through their crowns and sends a quiver down the row of poplars along the parallel road.

what are they doing?

'Calibrating.'

I can't explain that one. Her hands can.

bird wings

I remember the first time she heard birds, the first time she heard. Her astonishment at the raucous collage of noises as we arrived home from hospital to the rural squawks and tweets of endless avian conversations, to tractors being audible and not just feeling like earthquakes, to night-time harvesters, and to cattle calling for their slaughtered daughters. She discovered noises had to be separated out, some ignored, or they would drive you mad. I remember the first time she got fed-up with hearing, and she wished her deafness restored. It was, in part, but at least she had those sounds to lean on.

She treads the nest's perimeter, marking territory against gangs who claim ownership of ditch or hedging, who demand loyalty to dens where they wed friends in imagined ceremonies and burn their innocence in dares. I want to comfort her losing a childhood to childhood. Why don't I just give her a hug and a kiss?

We go home and I make tea instead, knowing she will read this one day and see the love inside my head.

Entry No: 19

Wind: *still zero*
Weather: *chill zero*
Outlook: *when he pulls down his mask I know visibility is not good*

I ask doctor about the outlook, if visibility is still good, how long before the front arrives? It depends, he says, forecasts are never exact. The blank cold of winter comes and my empty crown blends-in with new-found friends in waiting rooms, where we share frail networks and lend each other time. Three months, he gives, to my scarred branches. My performance coming to an end. I have not put it into sign or pressed it from my lips yet. They say I must declare it now but what if I have encores or hold my leaves like beeches? I hold the child tight to me, to keep me standing longer. Propped by memories and the futures I need to reach, I say nothing, not even hints. She reads my deceptions well. I see it in her book of metal-detecting inventories. An empty page, headed by a small ogham mark, recalls a chalked patio stone. When asked what it means, she cries and tries to move her hands to tell me but even they are not supple enough to describe what is held inside. Some things, I tell her, are just too beautiful and sad.

I take us to a wooded parkland, not so far away, yet even this place is in abeyance. It is so still that not even chimney smoke bothers to rise. It sits over rangers' dwellings, in a low frost-sink where callow suns barely reach. The cold seeps deep through bone and branch, crisping edges in its beautiful grip. The arboretum walk is an artifice of skeletons, vestiges of some long-dead botanist's collection. The Office of Public Works maintains the arrangement, re-planting isolated specimens. It is not unlike going to the zoo. Labels placed, trees evenly spaced, maximum aesthetic appreciation, and cut grass to sit upon, in permitted areas only. We are the only people here. Signposts suggest crowds. NO PICNICKING, CYCLING, HORSES, LOUD MUSIC, OR PUBLIC DRINKING ALLOWED. DOGS MUST BE KEPT ON A LEASH AT ALL TIMES and fouling carries a fine of TWO HUNDRED POUNDS. Must be a very old sign. Old enough to recall the shape-shifting water horses who do as they please, slip in and out of lakes unbidden, unbridled. Reason enough for NO SWIMMING and STAY ON THE PATH and it is reasonable to charge parking fees, stabling extra. PLEASE TAKE YOUR RUBBISH HOME and DO NOT FEED THE WILDLIFE, our café is open until half past five, unless a wedding reception has booked it. We see no one.

Somewhere, behind high metal railings, must lie all the forest debris. Brushwood, fallen leaves, self-seeding saplings, yet where are the workers to manage it away? The yards full of tractors, mowers, and supervisors of job schemes who keep the place running? There is so much work in natural environments. For now, the park settles, the trees all in repose. It is a wintery stasis, the world cold.

Black-knitted canopies gather over pathways, creating tunnels which lead down to a lake. The view carefully landscaped and crafted, held in aspic for nineteenth century watercolourists to frame. Not a duck or waterbird rises. Not a reed sways. Our breath stills in the air. Granddaughter skids stones across the frozen ponds. Each bounce sends metal chirping sounds, like polished arrows, under the surface. I wonder how much reverb she has heard.

listen   water screams

'You are not hurting it.'

it wants to get out

I have told too many stories of children waiting underwater. I am waiting overground.

'Let us perambulate around it.'

I spell it for her. It has the opposite effect. She races back and forth like a dog, livening the park, willing it to quicken. She searches for good trees to climb. She does not want the ones selected by park-keepers, not the appropriated trees with convenient branches at ground level encircled by benches for parents, although I could do with a sit down. She looks for the hidden ones. Some rhododendrons invade an area behind the lake, against the wishes of management. Inside their caverns she finds a riot of trees allowed to be. There lies between them a fallen oak. Some storm, no doubt, brought it down. Hollowed-out, with a few squat branches, it could have stood for another thirty years. Not long in the timescale of trees. The wind was assisted by some disturbance around the roots – a newly dug trench, servicing lake drainage. It could withstand strangulating vines, or cankerous sites where insects bite, and fungus taking hold, but not that. Granddaughter crawls inside its recesses and over its trunk. She touches the histories stored within its scarred bark and wounded limbs. It has the appearance, were it a person, of one whose heart has been scored with worries, and laid down to rest. More ennobling, even, than when it was erect.

grandmother tree   she names it   *skin like yours*

Thus proving that she does not hold me in veneration. Perhaps she sees, in winter's dying of the days, the natural order which I am avoiding teaching her. The slow rot already begun while all about sprouts the new generation. A small oak sapling fights for light among the rogue rhododendrons.

'What does the Grandmother tree say?' I ask.

I love you and I won't go away

There are no leaves upon the tall trees but in this moment, they whisper sestudes of comfort, and draw their signs across the sky, I am with you always and for the whole of time.

why don't the other trees help her?

'They did. She's helping them now, in her rot.'

how old?

'Five hundred, who knows? You'll come here when you are grown-up and remember me.'

you'll never die

I stroke the downy nub of a pussy willow catkin, before it drops its long tail and cries.

Wind: gusts 48-55 Kts, dir. 235° (SW) *immoderate*
     when really it may reach hurricane force with
     fresh to strong on other coasts
Weather: outbreaks of rain & drizzle, persistent and
     heavy at times, vision cloudy
Outlook: remaining unsettled, *relative flooding. It doesn't*
     matter, apart from the foundlings left behind

No visiting of trees today, just an urban line-up of alders outside Tesco. A regimental planting, in keeping with their proximity to army barracks, makes for an orderly presentation on a pavement. Although they would prefer much boggier sites, or riverbanks. They are young, and not yet extravagant. Twilight is setting silhouettes of industrial units against violet skies, but it is the alder trees which still draw my eyes, to the fairy lights glittering through branches. Silica bulbs ping off plate-glass frontage and sing in the hissy wind. I would sum the whole image up with a flick of my right finger, then two-handed showers, while making snaky arm movements. Granddaughter would do better, would make a great job of the weather forecast, could easily sign *moderate to rising* and show isobars closing in the time it takes to turn off the news.

Across the road, in between traffic lights, a rogue chain of red jellied berries swings against the darkened green of neat yew hedges, making a show of the Christmas decorations.

By the time shopping is finished, the weather has fully turned. An imitation hedge surrounding the car park bends and judders while faux green globes box against random gusts. The only other trees on this industrial estate are stacked in rows, packed and netted, ready to be decorated. One of them breaks loose and rolls along the tarmac, its pine needles silenced. Although the wind needs nothing to whip against as it fights itself overhead. Granddaughter sits in the car, absorbed in a DVD. I added subtitles. She turned them off. We have been invited to the annual children's party to see Santa. She saw him at school yesterday, last week with her Aunt, and she can't see the point of going out in the dark to see him again for sweets she can't eat and a colouring book for a kid aged four. I insist that it will be good. She might even get a colouring book, aged eight, and go to bed very late. She prefers her cloth-bound inventory in which she determines her own outlines and content. More recent additions include a joining-clip she found with the metal detector last week. The sort used to secure mesh panels together. She saw its potential and drew it as a magic connector, passing messages from one filmy sheet to another, issuing letters of the alphabet. She wrote both ogham and conventional digits. Like me, she does not progress through her book in a linear fashion from front to back but adds pieces according to her own system. The magic connector is somewhere near the middle, on page seventy-five, along with mistletoe which is very seasonal.

happy Christmas!   a welcoming party signs our arrival.

I have practised my response, hope that they do not engage in actual conversation. I forget my response.

hello   Granddaughter replies.

A man steps forwards, signs something else to her. She signs back fluidly, her meaning escaping me. There are none of our words in there, and she is so fast. His hands, on the other hand, sign quite differently, with a laconic panache. Not like the abrupt translators on the news. Although if I were to draw them, I could not ignore the nervousness within. It would be an edgy portrait, without his face, and all that intonation and pace. So much of him is talking, it is a lot to take in.

I did a series once, of sitters' hands, before Irish Sign Language put meaning into them, before I knew anyone who signed. I studied subjects as they spoke, not faces or body language but how they folded character into their hands. And their histories therein. I watched confident board members crumble their thumbs, directors shuffle fingers, and ministers pick over quicks already done. A homeless woman had warrior wrists, and a misogynist's hands had nothing worth recording. I recorded all of this in their revealing portraits, avoiding faces and taking information hidden under skin. Nothing seeps out quicker than emotion. Not only through gesticulation, but the tension and relaxation of tendons, the flexion of anger through skin, the bitterness of wedding rings removed and still pinching, the sadness drying in crêpey folds, liver spots poured over hard lives, knuckled consumption, sandpaper rough, alabaster unloved. The guise of nail polish. Swelling pride. I studied the stretch of youthful skin and laughter lines etched around thumbs. And I drew people's lives in their hands.

There is a pause in the conversation, the man looks concerned,

'I'm sorry,' he speaks to me, 'I didn't know that.'

I try putting something together in my head, about what was said and what they signed. What didn't he know and what has she said? I have too many blind spots, making sign language disjointed. I smile instead.

'Enjoy tonight, games starting later,' he speaks, while his hands fly.

She runs over to two girls from our Saturday group. I remember to thank him with my hand.

It's broken in three places, I want to add, to excuse myself.

'You don't look old enough to be a grandmother,' he says.

Which, unlike the same compliment when delivered by nurses, administrators, or admonishing strangers, stirs a long-forgotten need to flirt. How to even do that? I've no languages for it. I cannot be bothered. He is good-looking. It is in his eyes, and deep facial lines which tell of a life spent laughing. It is in his hands and in his skin. I think he signs the word pretty. That is, until he spells Granddaughter's name out.

'Is that the correct spelling?' he asks, 'Santa is labelling gifts.'

I want to escape to the toilets, to avoid mistakes, to hide my face.

It is but a brief sanctuary though, in cubicles for the hard of learning. At the sinks a woman scans my gaunt reflection, gives acknowledgement, says we met before on the ground floor of the hospital. I tug at my hands, not knowing the protocols of making wet signs. My incompetence is never-ending.

'Audiology?' she asks.

I smile in agreement, with no memory of her whatsoever. She launches into sign, bits of which I can identify but mostly cannot, and wish I had spoken instead of adopting Granddaughter's oft chosen option to remain motionless until further notice. I interrupt the woman to say I don't know that much sign, not enough to keep-up, to answer quickly. Fluency and readability adding to my difficulties. All those visual indications of meaning, tense, and intent, body movements and facial expressions adding sense.

'There is not much point in me learning, considering...' I say.

Her face freezes at my failures. I could explain, but it is easier being ignorant. It is easy when I have so little time. It is hard when I have so little time. I leave in time to avoid reproach. Or pity. In the main hall, the lights are bright, disco balls spinning, and dads are throwing moves to a mini disco. Children ignore them. Children bounce, po-go, swirl, and turn around the dance floor. Granddaughter's favourite song comes on and she responds as she does at home with an eloquent flow of arms, hands, and made-up signs transforming lyrics. A circle gathers around her, imitates her rhythms and shades, as they pulse in tandem to the music coming through their feet.

She is her mother all over again, the one who danced all around Ireland attending feiseanna in function rooms. She could turn her foot to any slip or jig, could tighten form and demonstrate accurate pattern. But her competing feet were prone to stepping out of the rules of traditional sets into ballet. She was known by judges to exceed the meanings of free céilí as her arms broke free of restraint and her team-mates followed her embellishments. She would flow into pirouettes and arabesques, belying her love of French choreographies learnt at the barre on alternate Saturdays. And even in tutus she would press Celtic heritage into classic Gallic, enthralling her ballet mistress. Always enthralling, gathering crowds.

The adults are signing. So many hands moving everywhere, signalling voices. I worry that their conversations could be private, or parts of a general discussion, or even a disagreement, communicated in simultaneous arrangements. I am too inexperienced to separate them out, know where to look, know when to avert my gaze, know when to join in. There could even be essential waves of information flowing through the room which I am missing, there could be relationships building, there could be warnings about the grandmother who never bothered to learn. I wish they would stop, talk one at a time, instead of making chaotic, rich, and quickly made signs. There is just far too much to catch the nuance.

my name is P.E.T.E.   signs the man who I ran from at the door.

I spell my name in sign.

'You look overwhelmed?' he shouts.

'I'm no good at this. This is how she always feels?'

'Your first time?'

'Embarrassing.'

'There are other classes.'

'It's so noisy. Hands, I mean.'

'Comes with practise. Parents are learning too.'

'How do I know when someone is talking to me?'

'How do you ever know? They'll look at you. Stick to one conversation, ignore the rest.'

'We have our own words for things. It works, but not here. And she's so fluent, I never knew. Everyone is so fast.'

'Loads of families home-sign.'

A man approaches us, holding a baby. He signs in a tight-handed way, compromised by his bundle. Pete answers. I can't resist leaning in to look, to get a response, to get that feeling all my babies ever gave me. That first rush when my new-borns' eyes met mine and they laid claim to the rest of my life. It is held in every black-eyed stare, designed to pull hearts in and fondness out. However long they may be with us.

The father carries on signing, clearly directed at me now and I ask her age in sign and feel pleased and nod and smile in response to his muffled hand movements. He lays his baby into my arms. I am filled with gold. He walks away.

'See, I could have just bought this child!'

'He's gone to the jacks.'

'I know the sign for *toilet*.'

'That's not quite what he signed.'

'It wasn't meant to be like this.'

'You can see your granddaughter's confidence. Your daughter would be proud.'

I look away, say it is shite.

'I need to see your face to lip-read,' he says.

I turn to him again.

'Sorry, I can't do this,' I say.

He tells me how to get home visits, puts a number into my phone, talks of extra support for parenting alone, but it is one long drone of things to do and applications and organizations and it all sounds like too much effort. Although couched in kindness. His softness throws me up against my laziness, my pathetic contributions to communication. It is all I can do not to well up.

The baby notes her father's absence and bawls, pushing my own tears back inside. I'd fill a pond, a reservoir, a lake, if I cried. I let it pour out some days, alone in my garden shed, wetting timbers and wailing in private. Still, some tears have escaped tonight. The father retrieves his infant, thanking and soothing and disappearing when he sees I'm a bit intense. If he could see my shed, so heavy with sorrows, damp with regrets. I must open that wooden door and let the floodwaters out so the Kelpies can swim once more as I ride bareback through the waters and cry into my pony's mane.

Pull the bolt back.

'Sorry, making it all about myself.'

'Everyone should vent,' he says, 'see, feelings can be communicated without being fluent.'

The disco speakers go off, music plays directly to hearing aids and headsets through loop systems. Part of the floor flashes rhythmic colours. Children pound, Granddaughter sweats, silent beats resound. I need to sit, I feel weak, mentally exhausted. Pete insists we go out for some air. Rain spits down into a small yard, shared with the take-away next door. A broken security light flickers, sparks fall from its wet electric contacts, and high brick walls surround the many oil drums left to drip their second-hand chip fat. There are many broken bottles. A sapling grows between masonry cracks. Possibly a determined elder, or ash. Either way, it has some stamina to push through all that, its sounds drowned-out by city clatter and rumble. He hands me a bat.

'Whack that,' he says, kicking a drum, 'and yes, it is shite,'

He pockets his hearing aids.

I tap an oil drum, test its mettle.

'In the middle,' he shouts, 'or you'll break an elbow.'

He has a plank which he swings back in slow motion to show he has perfected the art of destruction. And hits a drum, dead centre. And hits. I hit mine. And again. I hit the Mouthy Boy Taller Than His Trousers, the Teachers Who Never Remembered, the Parties She Wasn't Invited To, the Parties I Will Never Get To Give Her, the Weddings I Will Never See, the Preparations, all the Musts and all the Shoulds and all the Never Wills. But mostly I hit at Unfair. And we are both hitting and cracking and smashing, splitting the air with our unspoken rage and

it

is

glorious

Entry No: 21

Wind: *the gentle breezes of force 3 around a table*
Weather: *sun on winter days*
Outlook: *floral*

We eat Christmas dinner at the high table, feasting in a circle of high queens, winding our female line around each other. Along cloths of gold and silver hue, four places are laid, turning to five, six, seven, and more, for all the misplaced daughters and absent relatives. One for Husband too. It was he who had first suggested I make mini willow gift-baskets instead of crackers. We maintained the tradition, adopting one each. We now prefer their lack of sound, so that hearing aids do not suffer. Personalised, they tell of owners' preferences. Mine is lined with knitted Arran stitches, his with slate, one in tulle for a daughter who once danced, re-cycled ribbons for an eco-friendly one, and another with spray paint. Granddaughter has her mother's and, because middle daughter took one when she emigrated, I made another one for her visit, fresh as the trinkets we picked to fill it. There are edible flowers inside them this year, crystallised pansies and sugared violas, too pretty to sign. The four of us try with *frozen droplets, purple blue, tiny, sweet gift kisses* but miss their point. Which is love, sprinkled in their making as we anticipated our family gathering. Fragile moments shared. Richer for the two adult daughters who brought back signs from other countries. La langue des Signes Quebecoise flew in from Canada and British Sign Language sailed here on a ferry. We decorate our conversations with them, hung with foreign meanings. The child shares her latest inventions, those created to fit our stories of wooded lakes and trees in unlikely places. She has none yet for the sounds the willows make. Perhaps she would if I had not postponed cochlear implant dates. Perhaps it would be different, or not at all. I told them she is not ready yet and they said it was me who wasn't. She fills the room with her conversations. She winds garlands of fairy lights around aunties' necks to lighten their responses, make their lips easily read. She is glad of the spaces left empty at the table as she fills the gaps with her entire arms, talking in wide, rising, and descending sign. She fills the absences.

Entry No: 22

Wind:	*gusts in a vaccum*
Weather:	*dry inland, releif rainfall in upper reigions*
Outlook:	*poor. Saved by all the deities*

We go to the wild places, the Slieve Blooms, where mountainous strips slice through bog-land flats, and split Offaly from Laois. Nothing could seep through this border, not even loamy peat. Located only forty minutes away, it is one of our oldest mountain ranges and I feel cheated when I read that erosion already leaves them much denuded - to one seventh of their original height. They are the site of legendary histories, of tribal feuding, mystical monsters, and introverted poets retelling moody stories. I walk from base camp, up through The Wood of Slaughter, with my daughters and Granddaughter, all women, notice. Generations of females stepping over their lands, creating sisterhoods of herstories. They fought and battled and won hard-earned rights over these worn-down places. Druidess Bodhmall once swept her shawl over these mountains, shielding secrets and gifting them to another's son. Sharing all she knew, great powers were borne out of forest floor and escarpment. The oldest branches recall her Brehon laws and lore, write her myths into the winds billowing over Sliabh Bladhma, and sign their devotions. They were planted long before ogham stones marked her territory. Before her consort Liath Luachra stood guard. Liath, who stood for so long that she turned into granite pillars and Bodhmall etched her grey name upon them. Along with other branched symbols, spelling freedom for Mná na hÉireann.

It was hard to find the access road, with modern signposts being in shortage. We have long traditions of misguiding invaders, of steering them away from secrets. Now that we have found the valleyed forests and inclines, we can listen to their chaunting. The pine plantations sound quite different to the low-lying commercial forests grown on flatter landscapes. It is my first time noting that height alters their sounds, that bass notes rise with the contours of a map and altos sing through valleys. The wind, which earlier had been altogether absent from the day, along with light, colour, or any sort of weather altogether, now thumps down in heavy gusts. It presses over wooded crests with a wayward power while simultaneously managing to slither through the trees sideways. It is a noisy, busy place.

'Little precipitation, inland,' I say.

The hoary roar of water transfers its vibrations through the spongy forest floor. We head up a little creek, a detour, privacy for some wild peeing. Little one won't do it, is too embarrassed.

'There are no conveniences,' I whisper-shout at her, quite unnecessarily. I have caused dismay in her snowy white face, ruined the spirit of the day by insisting on stupid things when there are fairy homes in cliffs and waterfalls and the littlest of things to discover in this wild, wild park on a mountain. I appease her with some poverty biscuits found in my pocket, crumbly-soft custard creams which somehow got mixed-in with cheese.

it is lovely

So forgiving. She asks me why I am writing while walking. I have my blue notebook and pencil out, not quite drawing but describing an aspen previously captured downstream. You would think I have this already listed, but I have spent many a year searching for the perfect caricature of itself, one which lives up to its reputation. As each sample was rejected, the task became ever more difficult, trying to surpass unnatural standards. Under pressure to complete, even I surprise myself by selecting today's humble specimen. Dwarfed and bent by overhang, stunted by rock, it struggles to be an aspen. Moisture drips, snot-like, from twigs and this, I thought, is it, an aspirational choice. And so I draw its trunk reaching up in dogged determination, in thick dark lines so there can be no doubt it will be a hardy aspen one day. I draw the slightest of precipitation so that future leaves may quake themselves dry. I draw what it takes to make a tree beautiful. It is important I finish my project. More importantly, she wants to know who I am talking to about rain while I am doing this, talking out loud, is it to the trees?

say normal words that they understand

'I'm sticking with precipitation, sounds fancier than rain.'

Between us, we have so many ways to describe everything. Combining, altering, and adding layers of sophistication depending on the company we keep. We expand our vocabularies. Verbal forms spill into paint and plaster, dance, mime, and sign; our bodies transporting the emotion of information. Along with the lexicon written in our landscapes of rupture, dissonance, disease, invasion of ecologies, diminishing bio-diversities, and trees waving histories. Granddaughter shares my quest detecting these and adds them to her collection. Looking for positive solutions, she hugs a tree. A group of serious walkers stab their hiking poles past us. They do not notice, and she does not stop. She has her ear to the bark to feel what is being said aloft.

squirrel

I look it up on the sign app, recalling daughter's boyfriend being offered to shoot them, at twenty euro a crack. Grey invaders only. I scan clerestories of branches for leaping creatures, see none. Must trust that a squirrel woke from hibernation, trust the other language.

'Red or grey?'

colour doesn't matter   *tree hisses like snake*
wait

And I swear to god she makes up some sign which both intonates, and says, that the pines are brushing their sorrows against one another. No spoken words denote feelings quite as deeply as these movements of hers. I have tried convincing fellow writers to watch the beauty of sign language poets. She surpasses them in signing their loss. She signs the trees' singing. She has felt them and is winning in her understanding.

My other offspring, still here holidaying, are two hundred metres ahead. Already frustrated by our slow pace, embarrassed by our natural history lessons, they race to the top. Granddaughter runs to catch up. I was good at jogging, cross-country, ran frequently, along with the swimming, right up until recently. Well, last summer I suppose it was. The hiatus shows, I am an ambling rambler now. The track has narrowed to a rocky goats' path, with the river far below us. Trees cling to escarpments. I struggle to climb, clutching at slippery boulders, sticking clumsy feet in crevices. My heart explodes out through my chest and I am wet with sweat as my legs shake and I seek excuses to rest and catch my breath. There is so much oxygen here but not enough spare. I misjudged this outing, am not prepared for the stamina required, cannot get enough air. The sign said a one-hour walk, a leisurely after-dinner loop, graded easy for beginners. I did not consider gradient. The water bottle is empty, my hands dead from an enviable cold which hasn't reached the rest of me yet. I strip down to a T-shirt, decide against carrying layers and put a coat back on instead. I cannot walk one more step. We have already come too far for turning back and I fear I may die yet on this mountainside. Each time I catch sight of the girls waiting up ahead, they move on, out of reach, and I am three years old, failing at a game of chase. What keeps me going is embarrassment, I cannot show my weakness yet. Granddaughter runs back,

waterfall   hurry Nanny

I feign excitement, as it means we are only half-way round. We eventually reassemble and watch the hypnotic water tumble. Youngest daughter is unimpressed, expected a Niagra, and yet is capturing snaps to send to online friends back home enclosed in cosy living rooms. We stand enthralled by its thunder.

'You look yellow,' her sister says.

'Christmas excess,' and I make a head start on the path, hoping she will think I have been drinking too much instead.

Determined, I edge on, call on stubbornness, mind over matter, any last vestige of power. I cannot talk, of course, until descending. Before this happens, there is a long trawl to the uppermost plateaus. I am overtaken. There is more concentration. Then jubilation, the top! The others stop, applaud, lob soggy pinecones by way of affection, until someone screams that it hurts and it's not funny anymore. I am still straggling, stalling under the pretence of studying mud for its tracks of pawed creatures. Many have passed here. Some prints are too big even for badgers. I suggest it was something hunting, a predator of immense proportions. We walk on in silence, between seasoned towers and hollow shadows hiding deeper forest. The atmosphere changes. We form a huddle against unspoken fears and the weight which this place has suddenly acquired. It is holding secrets, I tell them, gateways to places where nobody goes. No wind brings singing to these trees. They were quieted by the beasts who came from far off coastlands and slew native tribes in the time when Sliabh Bladhma's sons and daughters were born of shape-shifting grandmothers. The wise women defended their mountain and suffered great losses but were victorious and made prisoners of the challenging creatures. Caged in the mountain forests, these enemies beat against tree trunks and clawed at impenetrable roots. Unable to escape druidical spells, wrapped in chains of ivy, they called curses down upon their captors. And they call them still. My story is ten minutes in the telling, due to medieval Irish spelling in sign language. We feel like running. It is already chilling as the light lapses. Instead of softening edges, everything flattens, and we must hurry back before dusk leaves us stuck in the spruces of Ossory, in the year of our Lord 1132.

Wind:	*blows ill again*
Weather:	*41mm of rain causes flooding*
Outlook:	*will continue to fade*

She tries the willows once more,
    hello trees
    and waits.

'They are not anthropomorphic,' I tell her from my kitchen chair.

I spell it for her, write it for her, explain. She shouts the syllables out, trots back down the garden, and translates the word into sign, waving at the trees. Or she makes it up. Either way, there is beauty in the way she says with her hands what took me ten minutes to describe. She responds to the shuffling branches with rustling motions and, if it is anything at all, it is a conversation.

'You need to come in, we've a lift to Dublin,' my husky lungs rattle.

She does not know I am calling. Cannot heed while her back is turned, while busy signing tonal patterns. The home help is late today. I do not feel like climbing stairs or getting changed or socialising. It has all been arranged. For the twelfth night after Christmas. My true Pete sent for me. Come drummers drumming. And share your rage with me. 'It will be epic,' his email read, 'come celebrate Little Christmas for the Deaf. You will be collected at 4 pm.' The transport arrives. No one answers the bell. The driver shouts through the letter box. I am alright, I can even let them in. We go as we are, passing the home help on the way out of the estate. Granddaughter warbles and whooshes with excitement, in simultaneous versions of voice and sign, commanding attention while I decline to answer. I sleep in medicated waking and wake in different places, slip between worlds and her gentle grip.

One moment travelling, the next chasing ghosts across imagined valleys where memory blends with fantasy and I need not know the difference. There is a party on the other side, in a stone ruin, to which I stride with the strength and pride of my twenty-five-year-old youth. Down the mountain incline, over sinking sods and river boulders I leap, and up the other side. It is a wild, heathered, containment. Revellers pour towards the sacred venue, for ritual, for something special. There is water, fire, air, tonight, in the ululating shapes which form words and meanings within sign. It is a floating language, rich and complicated by sedimentary layers and intuitive understandings from the beginnings of time. It is the ingress of something to somewhere I have not yet been, a journey yet to be taken. Yet it is peopled by past clans, a gathering of céilí mór with dancing sean-nós singing of shared genealogies in female lines. I watch fire splitting stone and am drawn to the heat lodges of chanting sisters dancing in concentric circles, their bodies enveloping mine and pushing me gently away, go back, they say, to your side of the valley, you are not ready. I have travelled so long to get here, I plead, but still, they insist that I leave them. They lift my knees so that I may walk. They guide by cloak and escort me down to the river. It is not much further, they whisper, go back to where you came from. I do not care for this part of the black-valleyed night. My return is not easy, hindered by the water where they leave me. It falls in great torrents and drowns hillsides in its efforts to detain me. I must fight the river to cross it. It has flooded five miles wide, hiding boulders and stepping-stones, banks, and grassy pathways. It has formed one large body, a silvery mass of fish, moving swiftly. So fast, in fact, they take my legs and wash them away in the great roar of water.

I reach for the tree-tops, for the trunks are submerged, and I swing in the tides from their branches. It is then the trees pass me, from one to the other, in a chain-link procession towards safety. Around whirl and pool and the dragging stares of herons nesting, they do not let me slip. They hold me fast in their grasp and when I look, I can see that their fingers are those of the frog children, and their eyes are made of glazed turquoise.

No Entry

Or weather

The party left me broken.

We stayed in a hotel for a week, to recover. Because a four star is so much more pleasant than a hospice. It had bog oak sculptures in the foyer, over which dripped sterile waters. The ancient forest ripped and transported, as witness to the treatment of leathered bog-men held under midland swamps, drowned and desiccated, nipples sliced in deference, progenies lost. Hair intact. I took strands of mine and plaited them into amulets, tying me to the present. I also bought a necklace, through room service, which was expensive. A replica golden torc for securing future transport through underwater caverns. Pete messaged me later to apologise, said he didn't realise it was so much effort. He could not read my answer. Because I never sent it.

Entry No: 24

Wind:	*0, far from all coastal waters and the Irish Sea*
Weather:	*grey skies, far from green*
Outlook:	*poor at GPS 53.101711, -7.153689 where I see myself*

Trees to the left and trees to the right once reached and touched in mid-air. In their sways, their melodies were shared, and symphonies could be heard by travellers seeking passage beneath them. A tunnel was hewn, for two long miles, through forest. And so an comhshaol was sliced, providing sides to choose from and mutism was driven through the middle. The trees will no longer be with us. They have reached merchantable height. Last month the diggers came and cut into their timber. Uniform stacks of skinned trunks lie flat on ragged lands. The remainder stand rigid, making not so much as a shimmer. I frequent this road often, for the hospital. They adjusted my medications so that I may be more coherent, for a while anyway. I've a child to mind, I told them, I need more than a while. We stop to watch, on the way back from today's appointment, and feel the ground shake at the quick take of fifty chain links, for profit. Machinery eats, walls of trees fall. Branches flail, thump, and reach back up in final gasps. No last words needed, they have said enough. Stumps are left, raw earth bared. A hare scarpers across ditches, chasing safety. We cannot feel its hind legs thumping warnings across the ground, there are too many competing vibrations. We can see it turn towards our road, watch as it is caught by a lorry. The harvest continues apace. Machinery stops. For a quick minute I hear urgent pleas from a homeless wood pigeon. Not soft, low coos but frantic, broken shrieks. Tractors re-start, nature mutes. Two men work a line, planting saplings at three-foot intervals, in corrugated plastic with supports, managing renewable resources. Granddaughter is crying.

they have no big trees to look after them

'They have each other.'

too small

'You'd be surprised. It's horrible at first but it works.'

I don't want to be like that

'Aunt trees will be planted. Two for every one that is new. Quick-growing silvery birches will shadow them, wash them in the sound of water and that's when you'll know the grandmother trees are helping. Their roots are still in the ground, reaching and touching saplings.'

I don't know if they can put up with it

'You will,' I squeeze her hand.

She points to a charred strip, twenty metres long, site of a lightning strike. It had killed a tree and scorched its neighbours too, via the very same system of roots connecting. It is not an explanation I want give her. The devastation will be too similar.

'Look, some bluebells coming up.'

She cries at their effort.

Every Spring we have sourced their purple seas, sought to wonder at their numbers under canopies hiding skies. Dog violets, primroses, saxifrage tufts; all formed part of our annual searches of new green seasons. This year's temporary hiatus will pass.

She is not convinced.

There are not enough trees left, or energy to convince them to speak.

I never did draw those lime trees last summer.

Wind: *a calm descends*
Weather: *into thick fog*
Outlook: *a soft day, considering there's no drying in it for*
                    orphans

Two small figures, Granddaughter and her aunt, walk away on a causeway of rich brown turf. On either side of their path stretch bare hectares, split by umber ridges, scraped into place by factory-sized machines. At first glance it is an apocalyptic place, with this industrial cut of farmed turf and the power station which it still fuels. Not today. Horizons have narrowed, vistas shortened as mists envelop, and fog dwarfs all thoughts of distance. It brings the eye forward, to the low willows left behind in the race to harvest three-million-year-old soil. Trees lean away from expected winds and shelter their younger brothers and sisters. Among them linger last year's grasses, blond from exposure, and this year's greenery. Colours are diluted by floating moisture. I lower the car window to allow the cold air in, to feel its watery rush. There is no more than a damp trickle. I listen. No sloping breeze to elicit pitch or tone, just a hush from the shrubbery, sonance blanketed. I must stay awake. Watch instead. I take atmospheric photos in black and white mode and upload them to social media. Behind me is a very different, and new, ecology. Here everything grows, filling ditches and mounds, disguising the vast flat grounds of peatland. This has been many years in recovery. Young hardwood copses, well established, left alone and unravaged. If it weren't for the straight lines of drains, you would think this was untouched land, that the top three meters hadn't been exported, or burnt. There are herons tempting, eyes connecting. Sinister twists of trees shift in the gloom, reaching tentatively into mist. Branches drip. Bog children lick their enchantments and other worlds open.

There is a fading of the bogs today, not just because it is grey or a Sunday. I imagine how I would have captured this as an artist, drawn nuances on laid paper or wove, rubbed and prepared layers after taping five meters square of Fabriano to studio walls. A panorama instead, in charcoal and graphite composites made from the woods themselves and carbonized in earthen kilns. Not fired on these bogs, which could ignite and burn for one hundred and seventeen days, flaming the turf and boiling the water. I take a large stick of charcoal and scribble fast, blackening a swathe, then change direction. Solid strokes are best, until hands ache from the effort and feet are covered in black dust. It is a day's work. Follow this with soft sweeps of a duster, bringing density and greys and occasionally erase where light escapes. Indentations left by underdrawings emerge, defining trunks and grasses. I forget bits, splash textures, repeat all the above and over-work marks until accidents emerge. Then I rub wet around the perimeter, revel in the gentle transfer of water from fingertip to paper's edge, watching it bleed. It is like an etching whose plate was selectively wiped, dark borders accentuating visual sentences. I do four of these, over as many weeks, each one sliding that little bit further into vague mists. Less detail, weaker, descending into softness until nothing is left on the last picture but the original white paper, its hatched and scratched surface the only evidence that something once lived upon it.

I do not have the strength for this project.

I do not have strength to hide weaknesses, make excuses, to find reasons to sit.

My two girls emerge from desultory clouds. Their sharp voices carrying across empty space, until losing definition, dampened by low weather. They are holding hands. Together, they will not sink; they have each other.

Entry No: 26

Wind: *fresh*
Weather: *rain*
Outlook: *lost between worlds which means there's not*
             enough weather left, according to Brigid, who
             stills the wind and rain

It has been two weeks since I drove over the straight bog road, transecting peatlands, connecting midland counties with its perfect Roman diagonals, on maps at least. There is no solid ground to anchor it to. Instead, it was made by layering stones over sinking wooden pilings, forever requiring further strata, while surrounding lands were dug out. No camber survives that, not for more than one rainfall. So, it was built to float, its humps and bumps rising with the waters, twisting and melting asphalt and tarmac surfaces. Sometimes cars fall away into cutaways. Sometimes ditches catch discarded washing machines. Sometimes sinkholes swallow all of them. And always the rain. It comes in sideways, warming Spring tides. My driver, on our return from hospital, ignores the sign saying, 'road closed.' Does not want a ten-mile detour at seven o'clock in the evening when he should have clocked off. He doesn't slow, he knows the changing hollows and flows. It is half-light. Windscreen wipers flapping, lights catching wet streams when he quiets the radio.

'Listen.'

The road pops.

It keeps popping in a rhythmical flopping until he stops the taxi and shouts.

'Jesus frogs!'

A sea, as far as we can see through the near-night headlights, of amphibians migrating, from left to right.

'All those little lost children,' I say.

We wait for the stolen souls to slide to the other side, but it is a never-ending tide. Thousands pour across the wet surface, lit and slick, breathing through their skin. Ten minutes of them and we are still watching, calculating numbers on the fifty metre stretch of road and they are not stopping. He edges the taxi forwards, squelching slowly, grips the wheel and accelerates. He is slaughtering frogs, not even stalling over somebody's daughter, over nieces and nephews once drowned. Tyres slap. It is the sound of chances ending. The sound of my child not returning. I cross myself, wishing I could kiss the scapular medal dangling from his mirror, pray to St Christopher carrying all ye little children over troubled waters, upon broad wide shoulders. Pray to Brigid of Imbolc feast days, who could still the wind and the rain, to goddesses and mysteries and wish that he stops driving over the comings and leavings of poor creatures in their sprawling, spawning limbo.

I cover my ears and pray to be deaf.

Entry No: 27

Wind: *strong*
Weather: *rain, temperatures rising*
               convectional rainfall = rain
               frontal rainfall = rain
               cyclonic rainfall = rain
               further rain expected
Outlook: *something in the water*

The Night of the Frogs leads to damp days of jellied pools, newts emerging under fierce rains. Or spitting, or soft, whispering, hot, only just trying, rain. Water, always falling.

Today we have the kind of rain that wants to make your day a bad one. It is down for the day. There will be flooding, silt spilling. The garden is filling with water, trying to re-join canal to river. We are slowly submerging. Concrete patios, cobble lock driveways, council pathways, all bubble and spit before marsh-water spurts through the cracks we missed. Peat dust in aqueous solution. I have taken to the kitchen armchair, to giving directions, to watching the living. I have left it too late to draw my lime trees plein air, to study them in location and find the best way to describe them. My compendium is missing this one last entry. I flip through books, scroll endless images of lindens, but they are static representations. It would be cheating now to draw from these. A jar of pale honey sits as a reminder of bees fed on lime blossom nectar and of a project incomplete. I could dip a finger inside the pot and smear it around a bowl, add a pan of lemon-yellow pigment, grind pestle into mortar. I could paint the summer into a page and let it stick the project together. It would speak of the child with her mother's honeyed voice. It would say so much. If I could do it.

From my chair I can see Granddaughter splashing

outside in her lavender wellies, pushing the tideline higher, slapping waves against the back step. It is only a matter of time. That too is slipping. I fish for hours, minutes, then wake and realise I have missed another bit.

willow swimming   she signs through the French doors.
willow likes water   I sign back.

She wades over to the willow trees and rubs her palms down trunks, as though horses' legs were growing there, their fetlocks cooling in pools. They would not be out of place for we have seen black horses descend canal slipways for old ways of healing in water, for hydrotherapy. Our county being home to new worlds of racehorse breeders, and old cures. Lead ropes on either side, horses paddle along, shapeshifting under waterways, where once they would have pulled boats. They do not neigh. There are no drays left to pull barges along towpaths.

We last walked the Grand Canal in Winter, when the sudden coming of rains on a leaden day meant hiding in storm drains and watching quick east winds blowing downpours away. Our concrete tunnel was home to many a sheltering creature, but mostly spiders. Their webs stuck to our damp foreheads, accidentally pulling threads which led to arachnid dens. She pointed to an egg sac swinging in the entrance and I vomited in the shallow waters. We ran, just about, along the canal, ears blasted by noisy crosswinds until we reached a copse of trees. There we waited for their woody lamentations. But instead of wind lashing through branches the trees only served to silence it, insulating sound. All I could hear were chaffinches' commentaries on the changing weather forecast. I spelt it out on my fingers, and she drew their duet, encircled in a tomblike silence. Now their habitat will resound with the sounds of sap rising, trunks vibrating as they suction liquids upwards.

Xylem and phloem having the rhythmical flow of a poem, one would expect those trees to function in stanzas or rhyming couplets, beating their botanical hearts out as creamy blooms of blackthorn close-over twiggy gaps and all those spiders hatch. Adjacent to those trees sits the rusting shell of a Golf GTi, next to an old penfold made of hurdles. I have never seen the containment of sheep there. It is far from roads or settlements, it is where soft grassy marshes compete with spikey reeds. It is where lambs go sinking and gizzards get ripped, and where landslips are common excuses when persons go missing over deals gone bad and monies owed. This is midlands' business, a place to avoid. It might well be covered in the white-green of Spring, but Winter lives there permanently.

Granddaughter brings an adze into the kitchen, left outside since summer digging, the wooden handle dripping. I describe its real purpose as a woodcutter's implement and she is not impressed that I would lay into trees, slay them.

'Is it ok to cut trees for firewood?'

no

'To make a chair?'

no

'Make armies to protect you from invading beasts?' she curls onto my lap, head ready, for the story of The Battle of the Trees, when forests transformed into armies who fought harsh battles.

'At the time of gibbous moons, when mushrooms smother beech trees with rank smells of dead flesh, and when blackberries are rotting, an ailing nation worries. The call of a hundred-headed beast rises on aching winds, a battle under its tongue. Children are hidden.'

I wait for her balletic signing to catch up, watch the flavour of my words transfer to her hands, and revel in her poetry. She continues.

Bodhmall enchants the forest   *she asks for help to*
fight the beast and the magic trees say yes

'They click, they stretch, they lift and rip roots from flesh and the whole earth trembles. Moles, voles, squirrels, and all those homed in woodlands are sent running from this mighty apparition of trees becoming. What do they become?'

soldiers

'A whole army arises. Not foresters or woodcutters, poachers or keepers, but military trees of the female genus. They sharpen their branches into axes and hatchets, they curve and tauten their bows, fling javelins honed from saplings. They have plenty and are very patient. There passes a thousand dames, ladies, and a prophetess in this first regiment. Their horses emerge from the waters, war tails swaying. Infantry, and an etcetera of timber foot soldiers join them, but their greatest weapons are their voices. They commence with a collective sharp crack, of hailstones smacking 22,000 leaves in marcescence. Then thunderclaps of synchronised jumping, as they thump forwards to enemy lines. Too many decibels in opponent's ears. The monster has too few hands to clutch all its ears. It suffers under their bass bombardments, ultrasonic booms, and high-pitched beams. It bursts into tears but is not yet defeated. It cries great rivers. The army has one last secret to beat it. The branches start talking, in sign language. Their wooden fingers swipe indigo skies with unheard words, so deadly they cannot be repeated. Curses and spells and hideous wells of lethal incantation turn black to red. The monster is dead, in the water.'

Entry No: 28

Wind: *light air*
Weather: *temperatures dropping before rising again*
Outlook: *feel like drooping*

The monster had a very unholy week, a resurrection. After Easter eggs had been hidden and retrieved from branches, and the willows had almost chanted greetings tied with pastel-coloured ribbons, I accepted the invitation to rest. Ten days, maximum, of respite, 'it is only a chest infection,' I said as I left. She signed goodbye, while keeping her arms crossed in a hug to herself.

    come visit   a kiss?   I asked, but she was afraid to give it.

    I assured her I would be back soon   *you must go out to the willows every day*

    She clasped our sign and cried a primal sound from deep within her.

    I drove out of the village for the last time, her utterance echoing through me. Her call to draw me back has split my heart asunder. She knows my body fails and demands my soul stays longer. The driver talks of idle things, of our village's statute acres and floating boundaries, its parish names and maps which changed according to invasions of armies or waters, about tithes being drawn according to demarcations and tidelines. As we drive further away the line connecting me to Granddaughter stretches and thins to a gossamer thread. It yanks and hauls, and I grip dashboards to steady myself against her pull. Driver says he hopes that none is so bold as to claim ownership of the ringfort, that its mysteries remain untouched. I know it is a gateway to other chapters. That it is not just a raised ditch enclosure, or home to a ring of mature trees. Its sublime image belies embattled pasts, layered ceremonies, annual pattens, and community gatherings. It is home. Some say it is where one goes to commune with the dead, to reclaim their bodies. I would often visit, hoping for this. It may even have homed St Brigid, standing proud with her sisters around the edges. It also homes frogs and the sounds of falling sticks. Not much to beat mendicants with but a portal, nevertheless. I made one last visit, just in case. Just in case I met with my daughters, that they were waiting, opening or closing doors to other worlds, that I may be admitted. I cannot be torn from this access point to families. I haven't waited long enough, I need more time to listen for missing daughters and if I leave now what will Granddaughter think, how will she know to go there and wait? I must turn back and tell her to wait at the rath. To wait for illicit exchanges to occur between the rath and the graveyard next door, all floating on bog waters, and to listen to the tunes of tree circles singing their cycles to the wind. Listen to descending fifths of abbesses chaunting in vaulted forests. They sing of the one and only noble tree, they sing of a time when we have different ways to hear. They sing with their branches, while making signs in the air. They sing of my children and they will sing of me. It is too late.

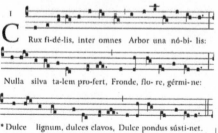

I left offerings of spring flowers on a headstone.
I left.

Entry No: 29

Wind:	*moving, slowly, upwards*
Weather:	*clear skies, visibility good*
Outlook:	*Valentia nearing a female line, woven together forever*

They don't give aspirin, just a pump which I am told to depress. Can't remember when. I ask for willow bark, to physick remedies, a nurse pumps up the bed instead.

'There, you can see the trees outside now. Isn't that nice?' she says.

It isn't, not in this position. I ask her to lower the bed back down a little. After cranking and yanking and, yes, I can feel all that, she gets it horizontal and level with the window. When husband was too slow in dying, we opened the window to invite his spirit out. He stayed for three more days. 'He can hear you,' the staff had said, 'hearing is the last thing to pass.' I imagined him floating away into the rose gardens, still listening to a wife newly grieving, to the woman he married after that summer in Valentia.

'Don't open the window, I'm not ready yet,' I tell my nurse.

Not that she needs telling. She is fairly expert on timing departures. I turn to look and sure enough the tops of trees are visible. Eucalypti, of course, flapping medically in the courtyard. They reflect off the glass panels opposite, all cerulean blue and illusions of forests. Out into that. They have the mien of short-lived trees, racing skywards, but can live for 250 years. So, it is not so lonely here. Husband had said it wouldn't be, that he'd be waiting for me, as we tried to pull his fleeing spirit back in.

Male voices in the corridor talk of ash dieback and discuss possible last-minute treatments, say susurrations are a nuisance, at this time of year, all that swaying isn't good for the ligaments.

I long for the child upon my chest, to tell her the stories of my days as yet untold, to leave the days in front of me for her to tell. She comes to me in the golden hours and morning silences, and in the shadows of her hands I read their purpose. She is not for withholding me but letting me go. I may visit the slate mines and stare into the light, watch droplets fall from dizzying heights, and he'll say that he loves me. Wasn't he right?

any news? I ask from my hospital bed. She looks unkempt.

there is frog spawn in the pond   gross   look I find
treasure under the willow trees!   metal detector

She puts her clenched fists into my open hands, turns them to reveal black rimmed nails. Her dirty palms hold the two precious frogs, unwashed and freshly dug. They have changed, into half-child half-frog beings, legs extended, their wateriness upended. They are luminescent. Their glow spreads up her arms and through mine, drips from bedding and slips through curtains, filling the room with all my daughters, lost and found. She lies besides me. I can feel them singing in turquoise choirs.

they don't have any ears   she signs   *they   hear*
through their skin, eyes, feet

she rubs their rubied toes   they just know everything
the trees tell me where to dig

what do the willows say?   I ask, and watch my shiny children dancing in aquamarine.

The willows sign and sway and sing about love but you don't need ears to hear the trees, you only need to listen

Acknowledgements

I would like to thank the following who saw the patterns within my prose and encouraged it to be shared.

Sean Campbell and Adam Bentley of époque press, who always know how to carry my words to better places.

My family for their patience when I cannot hear them, and my friends for being friends. My other two families are the writing groups Wordsmiths and Indulgers, who I thank for their generous support throughout the process, for taking my imagined worlds into theirs, and for such constructive feedback.

I will be forever grateful to Ciara and Claire for their early reads of the manuscript and for letting me know that I was on the right track.

The Irish Writers' Centre, Kildare Arts & Library Service, Greywood Arts, and The National Centre for Writing UK have all played a large part in supporting my writing journey.

And I thank any vet who bothers to learn sign language.